A Taste of Love:
From Sicily to my Kitchen

Marilyn Longo

A Taste of Love: From Sicily to My Kitchen
Copyright © 2018 by Marilyn Longo

All rights reserved. No part of this book may be reproduced in any form or by any electronic or mechanical means including information storage and retrieval systems, without permission in writing from the author.

Photography by Marilyn Longo
Book cover and interior design by Bean Creek Studios

Printed in the United States of America

Additional copies available from:
www.riversanctuarypublishing.com

www.amazon.com

River Sanctuary Publishing
P.O. Box 1561
Felton, California 95018
www.riversanctuarypublishing.com
Dedicated to the awakening of the New Earth

Contents

Dedication 5

Introduction 7

Appetizers 9

Dressings & Salads 13

    Story: Famiglia is Everything 20-21

Vegetables 22

Potatoes 31

Soups 35

Pastas & Sauces 43

Fish 57

Poultry 61

    Story: Memories of Chicken Cacciatore 67

Hamburger 71

Meat (Beef • Lamb • Veal • Pork) 76

    Story: Special Words 82

Specialty Dishes 83

    Story: About Olive Oil 86-87

Desserts 93

    Story: About Giugiulena 102-103

Treats & Drinks 105

Bonus Section: Breakfast 111

Recipe Index 120

Dedication

For my mother, who taught me so much, both in the kitchen and in life. My friend and mentor, Marrietta Longo.

A special thank you to Brooke. You were the wings beneath my feet.

Thank you, Anna, who named this work of love.

Introduction

Inspiration, we all love this word, because everyone wants to be inspired. Especially when times are difficult, the need for inspiration bubbles out of all of us like a dormant fountain waiting to come to life once more.

I realized this last year, more than any other time of my life, how I have been inspired since my childhood by the great family of women I was born into. My Mother, my Nanas, my aunts, to all these beautiful and strong women I dedicate this book.

I look around me and I see women in grocery stores shaking their heads, reading a list, and crossing out items. What they are trying to do is decide what is most needed to feed their families, and keep their budget. The stores are filled with tempting traps. This is not the first time in our country's history that difficult and challenging times have fallen on us. My grandparents and parents lived through the Great Depression. I always remember my parents, aunts and uncles, saying that they were never aware that lack of food was one of the issues. Their tables were always bountiful and the smell that came from the kitchen comforting, besides being heavenly. I find that description, like my own. Growing up our table was always bountiful and the smells and tastes from the kitchen were heavenly. There was no place in my world more comforting and safe than my home and the homes of these women I loved so much.

I soon realized that the heart of our family lived in the kitchen. The women of my life began in Sicily, Carlentini and Lentini, near Catania. They were widows of World War I and victims of the Padrons that owned the land and enslaved the common hard working people. They were my roots. I was told stories of survival and always between the lines I smelled the fresh baked bread, the orange salads, the pasta sauces and I could see family sitting around the table. My visit to Ellis Island put before my eyes the vision of my grandparents, both sides, coming to this great country, we so proudly call America. This land of opportunity for all. This was the America I was born into, I was taught from infancy to love my home land and to always be proud of my roots in a far away country. I have done this my whole life. Now I am going to share the wonderful culinary journey of my life with all of you. I know you will be inspired, comforted, and satisfied.

Introduction, continued

Though I learned a lot from my Nana, my greatest inspiration came from my mother, whose remarkable ability to love and nourish her family was her life goal. Her success was to produce generations of inspired cooks. Male and female. To this day we gather our families together with bountiful tables where love, comfort, and inspiration flows freely. Welcome to this part of my world, it continues to inspire and comfort each new generation. All who partake are wrapped in the love of those who create the feasts.

I believe that the greatest recipe ever made has these basic ingredients:

Recipe:

- *A lot of love (unlimited)*
- *A dash of inspiration*
- *A lifetime of feelings*
- *A cup of hope*
- *A pinch of luck*

Mix all ingredients together and create magic. You'll never fail and you will nourish your whole family.

— Marilyn Longo

Appetizers

"Beginnings"

**Time to talk, share a kiss, a story,
a salute to the wonderful aromas coming from the kitchen.**

Marrietta's Smoked Salmon

Marinated Salami and Tomato Antipasto

INGREDIENTS:

1 lb Genoa hard salami, sliced
1 container sweet cheery tomatoes, cut in half
1 loaf long hard-crusted French bread, thin sliced
⅔ cup virgin olive oil
2-3 TBS fresh lemon juice
1 TBS fresh parsley, chopped
2 TBS fresh basil, chopped
2 cloves garlic, chopped
1 tsp grated lemon peel
½ tsp black pepper

DIRECTIONS:

1. Place sliced salami in large platter with a lip.
2. Place sliced tomatoes on top.
3. In a jar combine all the rest of the ingredients and shake well.
4. Pour over salami and tomatoes and marinate at least 1-2 hours.
5. Serve with sliced bread.

SERVES 8

Blue Cheese Dip

INGREDIENTS:

¼ lb of crumbled blue cheese
2 TBS olive oil
2 tsp red wine vinegar
2 large cloves of garlic, pressed
2 tsp of grated onion
1 cup of sour cream
Makes 1 ½ cups of dip

CONDIMENTS:
Fennel wedges
Endive taken apart

DIRECTIONS:

1. Mix all ingredients together.
2. Chill until ready to serve.
3. Serve with above condiments.

SERVES 6-8

Hot Artichoke Dip

INGREDIENTS:

1 (8 oz) can of artichokes in water, drained
1 cup of grated Parmesan cheese
½ cup olive mayo
½ tsp of garlic, pressed

DIRECTIONS:

1. Preheat oven to 350°.
2. In a medium bowl mash artichokes, cheese, garlic and mix well.
3. Place in baking casserole and bake for 25-30 minutes.
4. Serve with crostini.

Condiment: Crostini or your favorite cracker

SERVES 4-6

Escargot

INGREDIENTS:

2 cans of escargot rinsed and drained
1 stick soft butter
4 garlic cloves, pressed
¼ tsp nutmeg

DIRECTIONS:

1. Mix butter, garlic, and nutmeg together.
2. Place dollop of butter mixture on bottom of escargot dish or if using small baking casserole place butter on bottom and escargot on top.
3. Bake in the oven 325° covered for 15 minutes.
4. Remove cover, place on second rack under broiler for 5-10 more minutes.
5. Serve with warm crusty bread.

Condiment: 1 loaf warm, crusty bread

SERVES 6-8

Muffaletta - Uncle Sam Noble's Recipe

INGREDIENTS:

1 large jar of green olives and pimentos, drained and chopped

1 medium onion, chopped small (use the osterizer)

1 large jar of porcini peppers, drained and chopped

2 stalks celery, chopped small

1 large jar Italian pitted green olives, drained and chopped

1 ½ cups of extra virgin olive oil

CONDIMENT: Italian crusty bread

DIRECTIONS:

1. Mix all ingredients in a large glass bowl, add olive oil to coat totally.
2. Put in jars and refrigerate.

This is a wonderful antipasto, served with thin sliced long crusty bread. Also excellent for relish on sandwiches, hamburgers, hot dogs, just plain good.

MAKES 2-3 QUART JARS

Dressings & Salads

Tomato and Onion Salad

Tomato and Mozzarella Salad

Perfect for Marilyn's Salad Dressing

"Salads"

As important as the main courses we produce.
The health in our lives.

Tomato and Rustic Bread Salad

As bread and tomato mixture is served and mix together, flavors become hard to resist.

INGREDIENTS:

Rustic bread cut in cubes
1 medium red onion sliced thin
3 cloves of garlic, pressed
5-6 fresh tomatoes sliced
¼ cup fresh basil, chopped
½ cup extra virgin olive oil
¼ cup balsamic vinegar
Salt and fresh ground black pepper to taste

DIRECTIONS:

1. Place rustic bread cubes on cookie sheet, drizzle with olive oil and bake at 350° for 20 minutes.
2. Slice tomato and place on bottom of large platter.
3. Place sliced onion on top.
4. In a jar, add olive oil, vinegar, salt, pepper, and crushed garlic. Shake well.
5. Pour dressing over tomato and onion.
6. Place bread on top.
7. Garnish with basil and serve.

SERVES 6-8

Marilyn's Italian Salad Dressing

INGREDIENTS:

1-quart size Mason jar with lid
Extra virgin olive oil
Balsamic vinegar
1 ½ tsp crushed Italian oregano
1 tsp cracked black pepper
2 tsp of sea salt
1 TBS sugar
2 cloves garlic, pressed

DIRECTIONS:

1. Fill mason jar, half full of olive oil.
2. Add oregano, pepper, salt, sugar, and garlic.
3. Shake until dissolved.
4. Add balsamic vinegar, fill the rest of the jar.
5. Shake vigorously until all combines.

Note: Test for taste, may need more salt.
Do not refrigerate the first day. Continue shaking and blending. Then refrigerate for up to a month.

Thanks to mom!

Green Goddess Salad Dressing

INGREDIENTS:

1 cup of olive oil mayonnaise
½ cup sour cream
3 TBS tarragon vinegar
1 TBS lemon juice
1/3 cup parsley, finely chopped
3 TBS onion, finely chopped
3 TBS mashed anchovy filets
1 TBS chives, chopped
2 tsp capers, chopped
2 cloves garlic, pressed
⅛ tsp salt
⅛ tsp black pepper

DIRECTIONS:

1. Blend all ingredients thoroughly.
2. Cover tightly and chill in the refrigerator for 3-4 hours before serving.

Marinated Mozzarella

INGREDIENTS:

1 lb sliced mozzarella (about ½ inch thick)
½ cup extra virgin olive oil
3 cloves garlic, pressed
¼ cup wine vinegar
Sea salt and fresh ground black pepper to taste

DIRECTIONS:

1. Place mozzarella in platter.
2. Mix olive oil, garlic, vinegar, and salt in small bowl.
3. Pour over mozzarella and give a couple twist of fresh ground black pepper on top.
4. Serve with lots of fresh crusty French bread.

SERVES 4

Fresh Basil Dressing

INGREDIENTS:

1 cup fresh basil, chopped fine
2 garlic cloves, pressed
¼ cup white wine vinegar
½ cup extra virgin olive oil
¼ tsp black pepper
2 TBS grated cheese

DIRECTIONS:

1. Mix all ingredients in jar with a lid.
2. Shake well till all is blended.
3. Can be stored in refrigerator for 2-3 days.

Wonderful on salad like arugula or fresh tomato slices. Great on any grilled vegetable.

Sicilian Orange Salad

INGREDIENTS:

7 navel oranges, peeled and cut in chunks, remove white pith
¼ cup of extra virgin olive oil
½ tsp of sea salt
½ tsp crushed red pepper (more according to taste)

DIRECTIONS:
1. Place oranges in bowl.
2. Add all other ingredients and let stand at room temperature.

Wonderful summer salad and a perfect winter one. Serve with warm bread, that's the Italian way.

SERVES 6-8

Raspberry Jell-O Mold – Marrietta's

Very festive!

NEEDED:

1 large jell-o mold

INGREDIENTS:

2 large pkg raspberry jell-o
1 carton frozen raspberries
1 small (8oz) carton sour cream
1 small (3 oz) pkg cream cheese

DIRECTIONS:
1. Spray jell-o mold with Pam and set aside.
2. Mix jell-o as directed using 1 less cup of water.
3. Add frozen raspberries.
4. Pour into mold.
5. With a knife swirl sour cream into mold.
6. Cut cream cheese into small pieces and drop into mold.
7. Refrigerate until firm.

SERVES 10-12

Fresh Tomato and Onion Salad – Sicilian Style

INGREDIENTS:

1 large platter
6 large homegrown tomatoes, sliced
1 Sicilian red onion, sliced thin
1 hand full fresh basil leaves
4 anchovy filets cut in half
½ cup extra virgin olive oil
¼ cup balsamic vinegar
1 tsp salt
Fresh cracked black pepper to taste

DIRECTIONS:

1. Place sliced tomatoes on platter, layer with red onion, anchovy filets, and fresh basil leaves.
2. Sprinkle with salt and black pepper.
3. Pour olive oil over tomatoes and drizzle with balsamic vinegar.

Fresh thin sliced avocado can be added; make sure to rub avocado with lemon to prevent avocado from changing color.

Note:
Tomatoes should always be room temperature. I never refrigerate tomatoes.

SERVES 6-8

Cooking Tip

HOW TO MAKE PERFECT HARD BOILED EGGS

Hard-cook eggs by placing them in a single layer in a pot and adding enough cold water to cover by 1 inch. Bring the water to a rolling boil and cook them for 8 minutes. Drain and rinse the eggs. Crack and peel them under cold running water. It is best to use eggs that are a few days or a week old to ensure easy peeling.

Vacation is the perfect time to reflect, and also cook favorite recipes. Now that's Sicilian!

famiglia is everything

A trip to Nana and Nano's house brought immediate response to our senses. We were greeted with hugs and kisses and the smell of warm fresh baked bread and pizzas and freshly roasted peppers.

There was always a Capricorn of vegetables fresh from Nano's garden. Tomatoes, cucumbers, banana peppers, basil, zucchini, Swiss chard, onions, oregano, and bell peppers. One of my fondest memories was a walk through the well cared for garden with a fresh cucumber in my hand, right off the vine. It was like candy to me. Of course Mr. Scarecrow greeted me with a friendly nod. It was strange because he kept the crows and the rabbits at bay, he was our hero.

I loved the end of summer because their basement was full of activity — jars being boiled and all the canning equipment in order. We would have fresh peaches throughout the winter — sweet, juicy and a treat on cereal or over gelato.

The big boards were laid on wooden horses and stratho — known as tomato paste — was laid out to dry. Cheese cloth covered the boards so the hungry fly never could get a taste — not so for us! I can remember lifting the cloth and running my finger through the sweet tomato mixture, thinking this was a little taste of true nectar. The holidays were a time of great festivity in our Italian family. There were so many good treats to prepare. Cannoli, biscotti, giugiulena, gnoccholi, casatte, and sfingi.

Desserts were always the least fanfare during the year, but the holidays were different. Baked goods became the thrill of the moment. I have often thought they were appreciated so much more because we did not indulge throughout the year.

My mother learned to cook from my Nana, after she was married. I learned to cook from my mother and Nana before I was married and it has been an ongoing learning process for me that developed into experimenting and creating wonderful treats for those I love.

Roasted Peppers

Vegetables

Fried Peppers

Stuffed Eggplant without sauce

Stuffed Artichokes

"Vegetables"
The jewels of any meal and always necessary.

Stuffed Eggplant – Marrietta's

This recipe is great for holidays and special occasions.

INGREDIENTS:

2 large eggplants (sliced ½ inch thick)
1 loaf day-old Italian bread, wet and crumbled
½ cup fresh basil
½ tsp sea salt
1 tsp black pepper
6 large cloves of garlic, pressed
1 cup grated cheese (use ½ for stuffing and ½ for topping)
4 eggs

SAUCE INGREDIENTS:

2 (28 oz) cans crushed tomatoes in puree
1 large onion, chopped
4 garlic cloves, chopped
3 TBS sugar
1 tsp coarse sea salt
4 TBS olive oil

DIRECTIONS FOR EGGPLANT AND BREAD STUFFING:

1. Place sliced eggplant in colander and sprinkle with sea salt, let drain while preparing the rest of the recipe.
2. Mix together the next 7 ingredients in a medium sized bowl (this is the stuffing).

DIRECTIONS FOR SAUCE:

1. In large skillet, sauté onion and garlic in olive oil till onion is translucent.
2. Add crushed tomatoes, sugar, and salt.
3. Continue cooking until sauce thickens.

DIRECTIONS FOR EGGPLANT SANDWICHES:

1. While sauce is cooking lets put together the eggplant and bread stuffing sandwiches.
2. Spread 1 TBS of stuffing between two slices of eggplant.
3. In heated large skillet, put 3 TBS olive oil.
4. Place prepared eggplant sandwiches in skillet and slowly brown on both sides.
5. Place in 9"x 13" casserole when browned (This recipe requires 2 casseroles).
6. Continue process till all eggplant sandwiches are prepared (Add olive oil to skillet as needed).
7. Once sauce is thickened, place over eggplant sandwiches in casserole.
8. Sprinkle with remaining cheese, cover, and bake at 350° for 45 minutes.

**1 CASSEROLE SERVES 8;
CAN BE FROZEN FOR ANOTHER DINNER.**

Stuffed Artichokes

INGREDIENTS:

10 medium artichokes, trim pointed tips with scissors, wash and pound open

FILLING INGREDIENTS:

1 (15oz) can of Italian plain bread crumbs
1 cup of fresh Italian parsley, chopped
6 large garlic cloves, pressed
½ cup grated Italian cheese, any kind
1 tsp salt
1 tsp coarse black pepper
Mix all ingredients together, making breadcrumb stuffing.

DIRECTIONS:

1. In a large deep pan that will fit artichokes (might need two) place ¼ cup of water.
2. With a teaspoon, stuff artichoke leaves with breadcrumbs. Going between each leaf.
3. Place stuffed artichokes on top of water in pan.
4. Cover and simmer until a leaf pulls out easily from artichoke.
5. Remove cooked artichokes from pan and place in casserole.
6. Put under broiler for 5-10 minutes, until tips are browned.

SERVES 8-10

NOTE: Of course, the recipe can be cut in half. I always make more because I don't want fights at the table, for that extra artichoke. They are also wonderful cold.

Beets Italian Style

INGREDIENTS:

2 lbs beets (fresh or precook)
1 small red onion, sliced
4 TBS extra virgin olive oil
¼ cup fresh mint, chopped
¼ cup balsamic vinegar
Salt and pepper to taste

DIRECTIONS:

1. If using fresh beets, wrap in tin foil, place on cookie sheet in oven at 400° and roast for 60-90 minutes until beets are tender.
2. When beets have cooked, peel and slice or cut in chunks.
3. In small skillet, sauté onion, olive oil, add vinegar and mint.
4. Pour over beets and marinate for 1 hour or over night.

Great summer vegetable or salad.

SERVES 4-6

NOTE: Beets cook at different times so remove as necessary.

Sicilian Vegetable Caviar

INGREDIENTS:

2 large eggplants
6 large green peppers
2 tsp salt
2 or 3 twists of freshly ground black pepper
1 ½ tsp garlic, finely chopped
4 TBS of lemon juice
12 TBS olive oil
4 TBS of parsley, finely chopped

CONDIMENTS:
Chopped sweet onion, Italian black olives chopped

DIRECTIONS:

1. Bake eggplant and green peppers on a cookie sheet in the oven at 500°; green peppers take 25 minutes, eggplant 45 minutes.
2. Remove from oven.
3. Wrap eggplant in a damp towel to loosen the skin and set aside.
4. Place peppers in a brown paper sack, let cool.
5. Peel the green peppers and remove the seeds and ribs, chop finely.
6. Put peppers in medium size glass mixing bowl.
7. Peel the eggplant, squeeze dry and chop. Put in glass bowl.
8. Add all the rest of the ingredients using wooden spoon.
9. Garnish with parsley and chill.

SERVES 8-10

This dish makes a wonderful hors d'oeuvre. Serve with crostini or sliced baguettes. This is a great vegetarian dish.

Stuffed Zucchini

INGREDIENTS:

6 green zucchini (cut in half long way, scoop out inside and place in bowl)
1 lb Italian sweet sausage, loose
2 eggs
¾ cup of asiago grated cheese
¼ tsp thyme or oregano
¾ cup breadcrumbs
1 onion chopped
4 cloves of garlic, chopped
Inside of zucchini

DIRECTIONS:

1. Sauté onion, garlic, and inside of zucchini.
2. In bowl, mix sausage, eggs, cheese, thyme, and breadcrumbs.
3. Add sautéed ingredients to bowl and mix like meatballs.
4. Stuff zucchini and place in 9"x 13" casserole, single layer.
5. Preheat oven to 350° and baked for 50 minutes.

SERVES 6-8

Broccoli Fugati – Mom's

Mom made this on the stove top. I discovered it is wonderful in the oven and less hassle.

INGREDIENTS:

1 or 2 bunches broccoli, washed and cut in florets
1 large tomato, chopped
5 cloves of garlic, pressed
½ tsp salt
½ tsp pepper
¼ cup extra virgin olive oil

DIRECTIONS:

1. Mix all ingredients together in a bowl, make sure broccoli is dry use paper to absorb water after washing.
2. Spread on cookie sheet in single layer.
3. Roast at 425° for 20-25 minutes.

SERVES 6-8

You can roast cauliflower, zucchini, asparagus, onions, carrots, beets, in this same way.

Mom's Broccoli With Sautéed Garlic and Mushroom

INGREDIENTS:

1 large bunch broccoli, washed and cut
1 tsp sea salt
4 cloves garlic, sliced
3 TBS extra virgin olive oil
8 oz sliced mushrooms (sauté mushrooms and garlic in olive oil until juice is absorbed)

DIRECTIONS:

1. Steam broccoli until tender, drain.
2. Place broccoli in casserole toss with salt.
3. Pour sautéed mushrooms over broccoli and serve.

SERVES 4-6

Roasted Peppers – "A Sicilian Staple Dish"

Roasting peppers, something you never forget the smell, the taste, the fun watching Mom and Dad roasting a bushel of peppers in the backyard on Thursday, Dad's day off. We were handed a bowl, a knife, and a place to sit. There were a few moans and that quickly ended when we were reminded of the dish we all enjoyed we would soon be eating. As a child you remember special moments, this was one of them, forever in my memory.

INGREDIENTS:

8 to 10 bell peppers red or green, roasted
5 cloves of garlic, chopped fine
1 tomato, roasted
½ cup olive oil
1 TBS sea salt (more if needed)
1 jalapeno, roasted (more if you like peppers hot)

DIRECTIONS:

1. Roast peppers on grill charring all sides, including jalapeno and tomato. Keep jalapeno and tomato separate and set in bowl aside.
2. Place peppers in paper bag and close tight.
3. When peppers cool, the charred skin comes off easily. Remove all seeds, drain, cut into a bowl.
4. Add garlic, salt, olive oil, and mix.
5. Add chopped roasted tomato and jalapeno for a little heat.
6. Mix all together and adjust salt.

Mangia!

SERVES 8-10

Fried Peppers with Tomato and Onions – "Bibi Cu Skoucha"

Spelled as pronounced
Translation: Peppers with skin

INGREDIENTS:

8-10 bell peppers green and red, chopped in chunks and seeds removed
3 fresh tomatoes, chopped
1 large onion, chopped
½ cup fresh basil, chopped
1 TBS salt
½ tsp crushed red peppers flakes
¼ cup olive oil, dash more as needed

DIRECTIONS:

1. In a large skillet, put olive oil in pan.
2. Add onions, tomato, and basil, sauté until onions are tender.
3. Add peppers and salt, cook until peppers are tender.
4. Add flakes at the end, more if you like heat.

NOTE: Wonderful with sausage on Italian bread with antipasto, or a perfect side dish filled with flavor.

This is wonderful mixed with scrambled eggs or fried eggs.

SERVES 8-10

Green Beans With Garlic, Vinegar, And Mint

Delicious hot or cold.
Wonderful summertime vegetable.

INGREDIENTS:

1 lb fresh green beans
½ cup fresh mint, chopped
6 cloves garlic, sliced
¼ cup red wine vinegar
¼ cup of virgin olive oil
Salt and pepper to taste

DIRECTIONS:

1. Steam fresh green beans until tender and drain. Put in serving bowl.
2. In small skillet, sauté in olive oil garlic and mint. Adding last vinegar.
3. Pour over fresh green beans.
4. Season with salt and pepper.

SERVES 4-6

Caramelized Onions – Marilyn's

INGREDIENTS:

6 large whole red onions, cut in half and sliced thin
½ cup extra virgin olive oil
Salt and pepper to taste

Directions:

1. Place onions in 9x13 inch casserole.
2. Drizzle with olive oil salt and pepper, stir to coat.
3. Bake at 350°, turning often, until onions turn limp and begin to caramelize.
4. Once this happens, keep your eye on onions as to not burn.
5. This process takes at least 45 minutes to 1 hour.

SERVES 6-8

NOTE: You can freeze onions in containers to pull out and create a masterpiece quickly. They are great on so many dishes.

Example: Use on crusty bread with gorgonzola on top of caramelized onions and broil for 5 minutes, as a substitute for garlic bread.

Eggplant With Parmesan Béchamel Sauce

This recipe is great for holidays and special occasions.

INGREDIENTS:

4 large eggplants
Olive oil
Grated Parmesan cheese
1½ lbs of chuck chopped
½ cup onion, chopped
4 cloves of garlic, minced
¼ cup of parsley, chopped
¼ cup fresh butter
½ TBS tomato paste
Salt and pepper to taste
½ cup white wine
Béchamel Sauce with Parmesan recipe follows

DIRECTIONS:

1. Slice eggplant ½ inch thick, fry in plenty of olive oil until lightly browned and drain on paper towels.
2. Place eggplant overlapping in a large baking dish.
3. Sprinkle with grated Parmesan.
4. In skillet, fry meat, onion, garlic, and parsley in butter until browned.
5. Add tomato paste and simmer gently for 10 minutes and season to taste.
6. Add wine and stir completely.
7. Spread on top of eggplant slices.
8. Make another layer of overlapping eggplant slices and sprinkle with Parmesan.
9. Pour Béchamel over top.
10. Bake at 350° until top is brown, about 30 minutes.
11. Cut into squares to serve.

INGREDIENTS AND DIRECTIONS FOR BÉCHAMEL SAUCE:

2 TBS butter
1 TBS flower
2 cups of milk
¼ lb Parmesan cheese grated
2 egg yolks, slightly beaten
Dash of pepper

DIRECTIONS:

1. In pan on stove, melt butter and flour to make roux.
2. Add milk and egg yolk, then slowly add cheese until all is melted.
3. Add pepper, stir and pour over eggplant.
4. Bake as directed.

SERVES 8

Potatoes

Roasted Potatoes

"Sicilian" Italian Potato Salad

Sicilian Italian Potato Salad

This can be made a day ahead and flavor is even better. Great for picnics and summer time fun.

INGREDIENTS:

8-10 medium sized red potatoes, boiled just until knife slides in and out easily, drain
1 cup Italian parsley, chopped
2 cloves of garlic, chopped
1 TBS of cracked black pepper
1 TBS salt
½ cup virgin olive oil
1/4th cup red wine vinegar

DIRECTIONS:

1. In a large bowl, cut potatoes in fours when cooled.
2. Add all ingredients except vinegar and adjust salt.
3. Add vinegar and stir.
4. Cover and let stand at least 30 minutes.
5. Stir again and serve.

SERVES 8

Mashed Potatoes Ahead

INGREDIENTS:

10 large potatoes, boiled in salted water until tender, drain
3 oz pkg cream cheese
½ to 1 cup sour cream
1 tsp salt
1 tsp pepper
2 TBS butter

DIRECTIONS:

1. Mash potatoes plus above ingredients with electric mixer.
2. Place in a greased casserole.
3. Cover and refrigerate until needed. Can be made up to 2 days ahead.
4. When ready to bake, heat oven to 350° bake for 30-45 minutes, depending if the dish is being cooked cold from refrigerator.

SERVES 10-12

Sweet Potato Mash

INGREDIENTS:

5 lbs of yams, bake for 45 minutes in oven at 375°
3 eggs
¼ cup sugar
½ cup butter
½ cup whipping cream
2 TBS bourbon
1 tsp vanilla

DIRECTIONS:

1. After sweet potatoes are cooked, mash in a bowl and add all the above ingredients.
2. Reduce oven temperature to 350°.
3. Butter a 2 qt casserole, place above ingredients in casserole.

PECAN TOPPING:
½ cup butter, melted
¼ cup pecans, chopped
1 cup brown sugar
1 cup flour
Combine all and put on top of mashed potatoes. Bake 40 minutes uncovered at 350°

NOTE: Whole pecans can be placed on top of dish to garnish.

SERVES 8

Red Roasted Potatoes

INGREDIENTS:

6-8 red potatoes, cut in chunks
2 tsp garlic salt
1 tsp black pepper
¼ cup virgin olive oil

Preheat oven to 450°.

DIRECTIONS:

1. In 9"x13" baking dish combine all ingredients, coating potatoes well.
2. Bake 30 minutes, roasting to a golden brown, turn once with spatula.

SERVES 4-6

Smashed Potatoes with Garlic and Parsley

INGREDIENTS:

5 lbs red skinned potatoes
½ cup olive oil
8 large garlic cloves
½ tsp salt
¾ tsp black pepper
2 TBS parsley, chopped

DIRECTIONS:

1. Cook potatoes in salted water for 40 minutes, drain.
2. Press potatoes in a olive oil coated 9x13inch casserole.
3. Drizzle with a mixture of olive oil, garlic, salt, pepper, and parsley.
4. Bake 400° for 1 hour.

SERVES 6-8

Soups

Italian Chicken Soup

Cannelini Ham Bone Soup

Sicilian Zucchini Soup

"Soups"

Comfort, nourish and fill your family with contentment.
Nothing can make you feel better except the loving hand that makes it for you. Be creative yet simple. The vegetables and other ingredients bathed in warmth will comfort your very soul.

Italian Chicken Soup

This transcends all nationalities. Can be served with cooked orzo added to the pot, tortellini, or rice.

INGREDIENTS:

1 large roasting chicken, washed and cleaned
2 large onions, chopped
4-5 stalks of celery including leaves, chopped
6 large carrots, peeled and chopped
4 cloves of garlic, pressed
1 large tomato, peeled and seeded
¼ cup parsley, chopped
1 TBS sea salt (more as needed)
½ tsp black pepper

DIRECTIONS:

1. In large soup pot, place whole chicken and cover with water.
2. Add above ingredients to pot.
3. Bring to a boil, skim the top of the pot as chicken will form foam.
4. When clean reduce heat and simmer until chicken begins to fall off of bone.
5. Remove chicken (can be served separately or deboned back into pot).

The following steps makes the soup truly Sicilian:
1. In small dish beat 1 egg and ½ cup grated cheese.
2. When whatever noodle you are using is cooked, add above egg and cheese.

This cooks very quickly and gives a special flavor to your soup.

SERVES 6-8

Italian Wedding Soup "A Soup of Gods"

INGREDIENTS:

1 lb hamburger
2 eggs
2 tbsp chopped parsley
2 slices wet bread "day old" break up & crumble
¼ cup cheeses, grated
4 cloves garlic, chopped

DIRECTIONS:

1. Mix all above together and form tiny meatballs. Set aside.
2. In large pot 3 quart sauté olive oil
3. 1 large onion, chopped
4. 3 stalks celery, sliced
5. 4 carrots peeled and chopped
6. 2 potatoes peeled and diced
7. 1 bunch Swiss chard chopped
8. ¼ cup cheese asiago "condiment"
9. ¼ cup chopped basil
10. 3 tbsp olive oil
11. 6 cups beef broth last
12. Add meatballs, simmer until meatballs and veggies are done.
13. Put in bowls and serve with cheese.

SERVES 6-8

Italian Minestrone Soup

The etymology of "minestrone" goes back to the Latin word " to hand out". It was a staple of the monks who kept it on the fire for travelers who stopped by.

INGREDIENTS:

3 TBS olive oil
2 onions, chopped
4 cloves of garlic, chopped
3-4 quarts meat stock
3 celery stalks with leaves, diced
¼ lb of escarole
2 TBS of parsley, chopped
3 carrots, peeled and sliced
½ cabbage, chopped
1 can of chickpeas
1 potato, diced
1 can of peas
1 (6 oz) tomato paste
1 tsp salt
1 tsp pepper
¼ tsp oregano
¼ cup of basil, chopped
¼ tsp crushed red pepper
½ lb of elbow macaroni

GARNISH:

2 tsp fresh basil
2 TBS fresh parsley, chopped
½ tsp garlic, chopped
½ cup Parmigiano Reggiano cheese

DIRECTIONS:

1. Sauté onion in oil and garlic until soft.
2. Add carrots and celery, sauté 5 minutes more.
3. Add stock and bring to a boil.
4. Add tomato past and seasonings.
5. Add rest of vegetables.
6. Cover pot and simmer for 30 minutes.
7. Add more stock if the soup gets too thick.
8. Add macaroni and continue cooking until macaroni and vegetables are tender.
9. 30-45 more minutes, stir occasionally.
10. Mix garnish in bowl.
11. Ladle soup into bowls and pass around the garnish.

SERVES 6-8

Marilyn's Cauliflower Soup

INGREDIENTS:

1 whole cauliflower (wash – cut in chunks and set aside)
2 carrots, peeled and chopped
1 large onion, chopped
2 stalks celery, chopped
5 cloves garlic, pressed
Salt and pepper to taste
Olive oil
4-5 links of Italian sausage (hot or mild) slice in rounds
Bratwurst sausage can also be used for a milder flavor.

CONDIMENTS:

Grated Parmesan cheese
Crusty Italian bread

DIRECTIONS:

1. Sauté everything but the sausage and cauliflower in a soup pot with olive oil.
2. Add sausage and continue to brown.
3. Add 6 cups of water to the pot bring to a boil.
4. Add cauliflower, cover and slow cook for 45 minutes – Enjoy!

SERVES 4-6

Jackie's Spinach Soup

INGREDIENTS:

1 chicken washed and cleaned
3 onions, peeled and cut in fours
½ lb small whole red potatoes
2 pkg fresh spinach
1 (14.5 oz) can chopped tomatoes
2 eggs
¼ cup of grated cheese
1 TBS salt
1 tsp pepper

DIRECTIONS:

1. Place chicken in 6-quart pot, cover with water.
2. Add onions, potatoes, salt, and pepper.
3. Cover and cook for 1 hour.
4. Add spinach and can of tomatoes.
5. Remove chicken take all meat from bones.
6. Return chicken to pot.
7. Continue cooking 30 more minutes.
8. In small bowl beat 2 eggs, add cheese, pour into soup and stir.
9. Egg mixture will cook quickly and soup is ready to serve.

SERVES 4-6

Aunt Grace's Lentils

INGREDIENTS:

1½ cup of lentils
6 cups cold water
2 stalks of celery
1 medium onion
2 carrots
1½ cup of canned tomatoes
2 TBS olive oil
½ lb bacon fried and crumbled or ham chopped (optional)
Salt and pepper to taste

CONDIMENT:

Grated Italian cheese
Red pepper flakes

DIRECTIONS:

1. Wash lentils in cold water, sort and drain.
2. Place in 3-quart pot with water and salt, cover and simmer for 10 minutes.
3. Rinse through strainer.
4. In pot, sauté vegetables, tomatoes, and pepper. If using meat add bacon or ham.
5. Add lentils and 6 cups water, simmer for 30-45 minutes.
6. Serve with condiments.

SERVES 4-6

Cannellini Ham Bone Soup

INGREDIENTS:

2 cups cannellini beans, washed in cold water
2 large yellow onions, chopped
2 stalks celery, chopped
5 carrots, chopped
5 cloves of garlic, pressed
2 potatoes, peeled and diced
1 (14.5 oz) can of fire roasted diced tomatoes
1 tsp cumin
2 twists fresh ground black pepper
2 tsp sea salt
3 TBS olive oil
1 ham hock shank bone (1 ½ - 2 lbs)

CONDIMENTS: Crusty Italian bread

DIRECTIONS:

1. Sauté all vegetables salt, pepper, and cumin in olive oil.
2. Add ham shank, tomatoes, beans, and 6 cups of water.
3. Adjust seasoning, maybe 1 tsp more salt and 1 tsp of sugar.
4. Bring to a boil.
5. Reduce heat and simmer until the beans are soft and the soup thickens (about 2 hours)
6. Serve with crusty bread.

Buon Appetito! SERVES 6

Tip: If you soak your beans for 2 hours in cold water, it cooks faster if you are in a hurry. But, a pot of soup on the stove simmering sends heavenly aromas into the air.

Zucchini Soup

Our babies grew up on this soup.

INGREDIENTS:

3-quart saucepan
6 zucchinis, cut in fours and chopped into chunks (set aside)
1 large onion, chopped
6 cloves of garlic, chopped
½ cup of basil, chopped
1 (28 oz) can of chopped tomatoes in juice
1 (28 oz) can of water
1 tsp of salt
1 ½ TBS sugar
½ tsp fresh black pepper
1 cup of cooked orzo (cook as directed)

CONDIMENTS:

1 cup of grated Romano
Red pepper flakes

DIRECTIONS:

1. Sauté onion, garlic, basil, salt and pepper.
2. Add tomatoes, sugar, and cook for 20 minutes.
3. Add can of water and adjust seasoning.
4. Add zucchini, partially cover, and cook until tender (about 45 minutes).
5. In a small saucepan, cook orzo as directed on box, drain.
6. Drizzle orzo with olive oil and add to zucchini soup.
7. Serve with above condiments in separate bowls.

SERVES 6-8

New England Clam Chowder – Kathy's

INGREDIENTS:

2 slices bacon
2 cups onion, finely chopped
2 cups potatoes, peeled and diced
1 tsp salt
1 dash pepper
3 (21 oz) cans of clams or 1-pint fresh clams
1 pint half and half
1 TBS butter

CONDIMENTS: Fresh parsley

DIRECTIONS:

1. Chop bacon coarsely and cook in large soup pot till almost crisp.
2. Add onion and cook until tender and clear.
3. Add potatoes, salt, pepper, and 1 cup of water.
4. Cook uncovered on medium heat until potato is fork tender.
5. Drain clams, reserving clam liquid. If fresh, chop clams.
6. Add clams with ½ cup of clam liquid, half and half, and butter to pot.
7. Heat thoroughly, DO NOT BOIL.
8. Ladle into bowls and garnish with chopped parsley.

SERVES 4

Note: Serve with warm crusty bread or garlic toast. This recipe can be doubled or tripled beautifully.

Sicilian Asparagus Stew

Sicilian Asparagus Stew

Mom's specialty – comfort food

INGREDIENTS:

2 bunches of fresh asparagus (cleaned & broken into 4 parts)
1 large onion, chopped
4 cloves of garlic, pressed
1 (14.5 oz) can of chopped tomatoes or fire roasted tomatoes
2 cans of water
1 ½ cup of fresh basil, chopped
1 TBS sea salt
3 twists of ground black pepper
1 TBS sugar + 1 tsp more
6-8 large eggs

CONDIMENTS:

Grated Italian cheese
Crusty Italian bread
Red pepper flakes

DIRECTIONS:

1. In 3 quart soup pot brown onions, garlic, basil, salt, and pepper in olive oil. Enough to coat the bottom of the pot generously.
2. Add 1 can of tomatoes, let simmer 15-20 minutes.
3. Add 1 can of water, let simmer another 15 minutes.
4. Add asparagus, cover and continue to simmer 30 minutes.
5. Add another can of water little at a time, adjusting seasoning.
6. When asparagus is cooked soft to the fork insert and soup is bubbling lightly.
7. Break 1 egg at a time on top – DO NOT STIR – you can spoon a little broth on each egg to help cook.
8. Cover and simmer until eggs are hard.
9. Ladle into bowls making sure everyone gets an egg or two.

SERVES 4-5

Pastas & Sauces

Red Clam Sauce

Beef Bolognese

Lemon Prawns over Linguini

"Pastas"
Oh the joy of pasta, craved by many and loved by all.

Julie Marie's Gnocchi

Handed down from Julie's grandma, Flo Nigro.

INGREDIENTS:

3 cups flour
1 tsp salt (mix flour and salt, make a well)
2 eggs, beaten (add to well)
Add ½ cup lukewarm water (add a little at a time, more if needed)
½ cup peeled and cooked potatoes, drained and mashed
1 TBS Crisco

DIRECTIONS:

1. Lay flower on large surface, such as granite counter top or large cutting board.
2. Make well in the center of flour.
3. Beat 2 eggs add to well in the flour.
4. Break Crisco into pieces around the flour.
5. Add salt around flour also.
6. Start to combine eggs, flour, and Crisco with hands, adding little water at a time as needed until dough forms. DO NOT OVER HANDLE THE DOUGH!
7. After dough has formed, sprinkle lightly with flour.
8. Cut dough in half, and half again.
9. Begin to roll dough out in long rope shape.
10. Cut in 1inch pieces, then with fork press and roll each piece.
11. Set aside on floured surface and continue making gnocchi.

SERVES 10-12

DIRECTIONS TO COOK GNOCCHI:

1. In a large pot of boiling salted water, gently drop gnocchi into pot and cook until they rise to the surface.
2. Remove with a slotted spoon.
3. Put sauce of choice on pasta and enjoy!

Note: Gorgonzola sauce is outstanding with this dish, see recipe on next page. Meatless red sauce is also excellent with gnocchi, see recipe on page 52.

Gorgonzola Sauce for Gnocchi or Fettuccine

INGREDIENTS:

3 TBS Italian parsley, chopped
4 oz Gorgonzola cheese
3 TBS grated Romano
4 cups heavy cream
¼ tsp kosher salt
¼ tsp pepper

DIRECTIONS:

1. In a medium sized saucepan over medium high heat, bring cream to a full boil.
2. Continue to boil for 45-50 minutes until thickened, like a white sauce.
3. Take off of heat, add remaining ingredients, whipping rapidly until all cheese are melted.
4. Serve over gnocchi or fettuccine for a delicious sauce.

SERVES 10-12

Cheese Sauce for Macaroni or Vegetables

Sam Bonafide (beloved cousin)

INGREDIENTS:

1 stick of butter
2 TBS flour
1 ½ cup chicken broth
1 cup grated monetary jack
1 cup grated sharp cheddar

DIRECTIONS:

1. Melt butter in pan, add flour, when rue forms slowly add chicken broth until all is smooth.
2. Add cheese, 1 cup at a time, until all is melted.

SERVES 6-8

Note: If making mac and cheese cook noodles as directed, drain, and add to cheese mixture.
If using as a cheese sauce for vegetables, pour over cooked vegetable.

Lemon Prawns over Linguine – Marilyn's

INGREDIENTS:

2 lbs large prawns
2 meyer lemons (1 lemon cut in 8 pieces, 1 lemon juiced)
3 cups chicken or vegetable broth
2 lb linguine
4 cloves garlic, chopped
¼ cup olive oil
2 TBS butter
2 twists cracked black pepper
2 tsp coarse sea salt

CONDIMENTS: Asiago cheese, red pepper flakes

DIRECTIONS:

1. In a large skillet, sauté in olive oil and butter, black pepper, and salt.
2. Squeeze lemon juice out of the 8 pieces and throw into the pan. Sauté for 3 minutes.
3. Add prawns, cook until prawns turn pink, stirring frequently.
4. Remove from flame.
5. In the meantime your linguine as been cooking as directed al dente, drain, add 3 cups of boiling broth and juice of 1 lemon to cooked pasta.
6. Place on large platter, cover with prawns and lemons.
7. Serve immediately with condiments.

SERVES 6-8

Clam Pasta – Gina's White Sauce

INGREDIENTS:

1 ½ lb linguine – cook as directed in salted water
¼ cup olive oil
4 (6.5 oz) cans of minced or chopped clams
7 cloves of garlic, pressed
1 qt heavy whipping cream
¼ tsp of red pepper flakes, add more if desired
1 TBS flour
¼ cup Italian parsley, chopped

CONDIMENTS: Grated Italian asiago cheese, red pepper flakes

DIRECTIONS:

1. Drain clams and reserve the juice.
2. In a large skillet, put olive oil, garlic, drained clams, pepper flakes, sauté for 5 minutes.
3. To the reserved juice add flour and dissolve so there are no lumps.
4. Add to sauté clams and bring to a boil, mixture will slightly thicken.
5. Slowly add cream, continue cooking until pasta is done.
6. Put on platter, pour sauce over, sprinkle with parsley.

SERVES 6

Brother Jo Jo's Original Clam Pasta

INGREDIENTS:

1 cup of olive oil
2 large tomatoes, chopped and set aside
10 cloves garlic, sliced
1 bunch Italian parsley, chopped
1 hand full fresh basil, chopped
1 (51 oz) can Gorton's Chef Style clams
1 cup sherry, divided in half
Salt and pepper to taste
½ tsp red pepper flakes
2 lb linguine, cook as directed in salted water al dente

DIRECTIONS:

1. In large skillet, brown garlic in olive oil adding parsley, basil, and drained clams reserving juice.
2. Add ½ cup sherry, then the juice of the clams.
3. Add salt, pepper, and red pepper flakes.
4. Cook for 10-15 minutes.
5. When pasta is cooked, drain and place on platter.
6. Add remaining sherry to sauce, mixing thoroughly.
7. Pour over pasta.
8. Put chopped tomatoes on top and serve.

SERVES 6-8

Clam Sauce – Red

INGREDIENTS:

3 (6 oz) cans chopped or whole clams (reserve juice)
6-8 cloves garlic, chopped
½ cup basil, chopped
6 TBS olive oil
2 (28 oz) cans crushed tomatoes
2 TBS sugar
1 tsp salt
1 tsp black pepper
½ cup white wine
1 lb pasta of choice

CONDIMENTS: Red pepper flakes, grated asiago cheese

DIRECTIONS:

1. Sauté clams, garlic, and basil in olive oil for 5 minutes and remove from heat.
2. In separate saucepan mix all liquid ingredients.
3. Add sugar, salt, and pepper to taste. Bring to a boil, reduce heat.
4. Add all sautéed ingredients and let simmer 30-40 minutes.
5. While sauce is cooking, prepare pasta according to directions.
6. Drain pasta, place in platter.
7. Add sauce, serve with condiments.

SERVES 4 AS MAIN DISH

Fettuccine Primavera

Cousin Sam Bonafide from Salvatori's Restaurant, Omaha Nebraska

INGREDIENTS:

2 lb fettuccine, cooked as directed al dente
1 cup broccoli, chopped small
1 cup zucchini, chopped small
1 cup asparagus, chopped small
1 small onion, chopped fine
5 mushrooms sliced thin
1 cup Italian green beans, chopped small
4 cloves of garlic, chopped fine
1 cup frozen peas
¼ cup olive oil
4 TBS butter
2 TBS pesto (see recipe on page 53)
1 TBS flour
2 cups heavy whipping cream
½ cup chopped prosciutto
½ cup white wine
½ cup fontinella cheese
½ cup Romano

DIRECTIONS:

1. In large skillet, sauté all vegetables in olive oil and 2 TBS butter.
2. Add peas last and pesto.
3. Mix all together and set aside.
4. In saucepan, make béchamel cream sauce with flour and 2 TBS butter, making a roux.
5. Slowly add heavy whipping cream until smooth.
6. Add chopped prosciutto.
7. Add wine.
8. Fold in fontinella and Romano until all cheese is melted.
9. Fold in prepared vegetables.
10. Serve over buttered fettuccine noodles.

SERVES 10-12

Note: Delicious served with chardonnay or pinot grigio.

Angie Noble's Famous Meat Ravioli

Angie was one of my mother's best friends. Her husband Subby and my father Joe were also good friends, so much so that they traveled every year together to Padre Island. All four were originally from Little Italy.

NEEDED:

Pasta machine
Ravioli cutter

INGREDIENTS FOR DOUGH:

6 heaping cups flour
6 eggs
1 ½ cup of hot water (approximately)
This is the dough. After mixing dough by hand, soft not sticky, let it stand covered for 30 minutes. Cut into pieces and roll on pasts machine starting with number 1 and ended with number 5.

INGREDIENTS FOR FILLING:

3-4 fresh green onions
2 lbs of ground round
1 stick of butter
½ cup of parsley, chopped
Sauté the above ingredients together and drain.
Add 1 small can of tomato past to the above.
Salt and pepper to taste.
Stir until all is blended.
Remove from heat and let cool.
Add 1 cup of cheese and 1 beaten egg.

DIRECTIONS:

1. Beat 1 egg and spread lightly on the bottom strip of dough.
2. Then take small mounds of hamburger mixture and place in row on dough.
3. Then lay top dough over mounds, slightly pat dough around mounds with hands.
4. Use ravioli cutter and cut.
5. When cooking ravioli boil water in a large pasta pot.
6. Drop in frozen ravioli to boiling water and cook 30 minutes. DO NOT STIR! (If not frozen be sure they are dry. Cooking time will be 15 minutes).

MAKES 75 RAVIOLI – 6 PER SERVING

Note: Ravioli can be frozen until ready to use.

Marrietta's Pot of Sugo

INGREDIENTS:

1 large pot
6 (28.5 oz) cans crushed tomatoes
3 (6 oz) cans tomato paste and 3 cans of water
4 (11.5 oz) cans tomato sauce
Put tomato paste in large pot and dissolve with 3 cans of hot water. Add crushed tomatoes and tomato sauce.

ADD TO POT THE FOLLOWING:

1. 3 bay leaves
2. 5 whole cloves
3. Sugar – 1 TBS for every can of tomatoes and tomato sauce
4. 2 TBS salt
5. 1 TBS pepper

IN A LARGE SKILLET, BROWN THE FOLLOWING:

1. 4 large onions, chopped
2. 1 bulb garlic, pressed
3. ½ cup fresh basil, chopped
4. Set aside

IN THE SAME SKILLET, BROWN THE FOLLOWING:

1. 3 lbs ox tails and or pork neck bones
2. Season with salt and pepper
3. Place with onion, garlic, and basil in large bowl and set aside.
4. Note: You can add the following as was often in our pot of Sugo according to our Sicilian tradition:
   - Pigtails boiled and drained in salted water
   - Chicken feet boiled and drained in salted water

Put ingredients that you have set aside into the pot of sauce, which you have brought to a low simmer.

SERVES 20
This is made to freeze. Add meatballs from page 71.

 "SUGO AND POPETTI"
SPAGHETTI AND MEATBALLS

I remember as a small child the smell of onions, garlic, and basil sautéing, the aroma is like no other. Tomatoes boiling being peeled, drained and squeezed into a large pot on the stove. In a skillet, pork or beef neck bones were browned- meatballs were being formed and the marriage made in heaven was about to take place.

Lucky me! I was there for its beginning and learned how to create forever!!! Thank you, Nana.

Aunt Flo Nigro's Ricotta Ravioli

INGREDIENTS:

6 cups of flour (DO NOT PACK)
1 tsp salt
2 heaping TBS Crisco
4 eggs, beat with fork
1 ½ – 2 cups lukewarm water
This is the dough. After mixing dough by hand, soft not sticky, let it stand covered for 30 minutes. Cut into pieces and roll on pasts machine starting with number 1 and ended with number 5.

INGREDIENTS FOR FILLING:

2 lbs ricotta
2 eggs, beat with fork
½ to ¾ cup grated cheese
¾ cup of Italian parsley, chopped
Mix the above ingredients together by hand until smooth.

DIRECTIONS:

1. Beat 1 egg and spread lightly on the bottom strip of dough.
2. Place 1 TBS of ricotta filling in mounds on strip.
3. Then lay top dough over mounds, slightly pat dough around mounds with hands.
4. Use ravioli cutter and cut.
5. When cooking ravioli boil water in a large pasta pot.
6. Drop in frozen ravioli to boiling water and cook 30 minutes. DO NOT STIR! (If not frozen be sure they are dry. Cooking time will be 15 minutes).

MAKES 75 RAVIOLI – 4-5 PER SERVING

Note: Ravioli can be frozen until ready to use. Place ravioli on well floured large cookie sheet as a bottom layer. Place wax paper on top and layer again with ravioli. Continue and freeze. Once frozen, ravioli can be put in large freezer plastic bags until use.

Sasa "Quick Sauce" – Meatless

INGREDIENTS:

3 (28 oz) cans of crushed tomatoes
6 large cloves of garlic, chopped
1 cup fresh basil, chopped
¼ cup extra virgin olive oil
Salt and pepper to taste
3 TBS sugar
1 dried red chili pepper
Note: If using fresh tomatoes, more sugar may be required if tomatoes are tart

DIRECTIONS:

1. Sauté garlic, olive oil, and basil. Do not let garlic brown.
2. Add tomatoes, sugar, salt and pepper.
3. Let simmer at low boil for 30 minutes.
4. In the mean time, cook pasta in salted water as directed.
5. Pour sauce over pasta and serve with asiago cheese.

1 LB SERVES 4-6; 2 LB SERVES 6-8

Note: If sauce seems to thick add a little water from the pasta pot.

Vodka Cream Pasta Sauce

INGREDIENTS:

1 small onion, minced
4 garlic cloves, chopped
¼ cup basil, chopped
1 tsp salt
1 TBS sugar
4 TBS olive oil
1 cup vodka
3 cups crushed tomatoes in puree
½ cup half and half or heavy cream
1 lb pasta (fettuccine or pasta of choice)

DIRECTIONS:

1. Sauté onion, garlic, basil, in olive oil.
2. Add tomatoes and vodka.
3. Simmer 20-25 minutes.
4. Add half and half or cream, blend well and do not boil.
5. Cook pasta according to directions.
6. Pour sauce over pasta and serve immediately.

SERVES 4-6

Aunt Josie's Pesto Basil Sauce

INGREDIENTS:

2 cups of packed basil
8 cloves of garlic
½ cup of pine nuts (walnuts can be substituted)
½ cup of grated Parmesan
1 cup of olive oil

DIRECTIONS:

1. Put all ingredients in blender except for cheese and olive oil.
2. Gradually add oil into blender as you pulverize.
3. Add cheese, this will make your pesto paste.
4. This pesto can be used over pasta, fish, chicken, and vegetables as desired.

OPTION:

Creamy pesto sauce

INGREDIENTS:

½ cup half and half
1 TBS corn starch
¼ cup warm water

DIRECTIONS:

5. Mix cornstarch and water till dissolved.
6. In small saucepan, add half and half plus step 1.
7. Heat too just before boiling, cream will thicken.
8. Add to pesto recipe for creamy pesto sauce.

SERVES 8-10

Note: This is delicious also on gnocchi.

Spaghetti Carbonara

INGREDIENTS:

1 lb spaghetti
2 TBS salt
4-6 quarts boiling water
½ cup butter
½ lb of bacon or pancetta, chopped
1 large onion, chopped
3 cloves of garlic, chopped
½ lb of mushrooms sliced
½ cup of white wine
½ pint of heavy cream
2 eggs (well beaten)
¼ cup Italian parsley chopped

CONDIMENT: Grated cheese

DIRECTIONS:

1. While pasta is cooking melt butter in large skillet and sauté bacon until golden brown.
2. Add onion and garlic, sauté 5 more minutes.
3. Add mushrooms, stir in wine, continue cooking until half of the liquid is absorbed.
4. Beat the cream and eggs until blended.
5. Stir mixture into skillet.
6. Drain pasta, add to sauce and stir over low heat.
7. Add parsley and serve with grated cheese.

SERVES 4-6

Note: I always reserve salted pasta water in case sauce is too thick.

Marilyn's Stuffed Manicotti

So delicious!

NEEDED:

2 boxes manicotti shells
(found in pasta section)
Recipe for meat bolognese sauce
(refer to page 55)

INGREDIENTS FOR MEAT FILLING:

1 lb lean ground beef
1 large onion, chopped
1 TBS olive oil
1 large pkg of fresh spinach cleaned and ready to use
¼ cup of grated parmesan cheese
2 eggs, slightly beaten
Salt and pepper to taste
This fills 8 shells

DIRECTIONS FOR MEAT FILLING:

1. Brown ground beef and onion in 1 TBS olive oil.
2. Drain excess grease.
3. Add spinach, cheese, salt, and pepper until spinach is wilted.
4. Remove from heat and let cool.
5. Add eggs and mix well.
6. Stuff mixture into shells. Make sure the entire shell is filled with meat and spinach filling.

* A long spoon helps to fill the shell.

INGREDIENTS FOR RICOTTA FILLING:

1 lb of ricotta
1 egg, beaten
3 TBS Italian parsley, minced
¼ cup of grated parmesan cheese
2 TBS fresh basil, chopped
½ tsp nutmeg
½ tsp salt
¼ tsp pepper
This fills 8 shells.

DIRECTIONS FOR RICOTTA FILLING:

1. Mix the above ingredients together in a large bowl.
2. Stuff mixture into shells.

BAKING DIRECTIONS:

1. Place bolognese sauce on bottom of 9"x13" casserole.
2. Place stuffed Manicotti on top of sauce leaving space between each shell for expansion.
3. Cover with bolognese sauce.
4. Add ½ cup of water to casserole.
5. Cover with foil and bake at 375° for 1 hour.
6. Serve with remaining bolognese sauce and grated cheese.

SERVES 8

Marilyn's Meat Bolognese

6-quart pan needed

INGREDIENTS:

3 ½ lb of lean ground beef
5 cloves garlic, pressed
1 large onion, chopped
1 cup basil, chopped
2 pinches of sea salt
1 twist of ground black pepper
3 (28 oz) cans of chopped tomatoes
1 (28 oz) can of ground tomatoes in puree
6 whole cloves
2 whole bay leaves
1 pinch Italian dried oregano
4 large pinches of salt to taste
½ cup of sugar

DIRECTIONS:

1. Sauté first 6 ingredients in 6-quart pot till no pink remains on hamburger.
2. Add ingredients 7-13 to pot.
3. Let cook at low boil for 1 hour or 1 and half hours.

YIELDS ENOUGH FOR 15 PEOPLE OR MORE
Freeze in containers for another great meal if you are cooking for less.

1 LB OF PASTA SERVES 4-6
Penne rigatoni and mostaccioli collect the sauce well and are best with this bolognese.

Sausage Bolognese

INGREDIENTS:

1 lb spicy or mild Italian sausage, no casing
5 cloves garlic, pressed
2 heaping TBS tomato paste
1 (28 oz) can crushed tomatoes in puree
2 TBS red wine vinegar
½ tsp salt
1 tsp sugar
½ cup grated Parmigiano Reggiano
1 lb rigatoni pasta

DIRECTIONS:

1. Sauté sausage and garlic in skillet, drain some of the grease.
2. Add tomato paste, crushed tomatoes, vinegar, salt, and sugar.
3. Continue cooking 30 minutes.
4. Add grated cheese stirring in completely.
5. Pour over pasta and serve with more grated cheese.

SERVES 4-6

Note: Sauce can be made while rigatoni is cooking
Quick and easy! Always delicious!

Pasta With Anchovies — Aunt Flo Nigro

INGREDIENTS:

¼ cup olive oil
1 lb thin pasta or my favorite perciatelli
5 cloves of garlic, minced
1 can of anchovy filets with oil minced
3 TBS parsley, minced
Red pepper flakes or fresh ground black pepper
½ cup salted pasta water

CONDIMENTS: Grated cheese, homemade breadcrumbs (see recipe below)

DIRECTIONS:

1. Heat 2 TBS of olive oil in skillet, over moderate heat.
2. Add garlic sauté 1 minute.
3. Add anchovies and sauté with wooden spoon until dissolved.
4. Add parsley and season with pepper and salt if needed
5. Cook pasta as directed.
6. When pasta is done, drain, reserving ½ cup of pasta water add to anchovy mixture.
7. Immediately toss with pasta.
8. Pass the condiments.

1 LB PASTA SERVES 4-6

BREADCRUMBS

INGREDIENTS:

⅓ cup of plain breadcrumbs
2 tsp olive oil
¼ tsp salt

DIRECTIONS:

1. In small skillet, place olive oil on medium heat, add breadcrumbs and salt, sautéing constantly until golden brown.
2. Transfer to a small bowl and let cool.
3. Serve as a condiment.

Fish

Fresh sand dabs made the Sicilian way

And sometimes we dance while we cook!

Marinated Crab

"Fish"

And they thanked the heavens for its abundance.

Sicilian White Fish in Light Tomato Sauce

This dish was served customarily on Christmas Eve.

INGREDIENTS:

1 ½ lb whiting fish or any solid white fish
1 large onion, chopped
6 cloves garlic, chopped
¼ cup parsley, chopped
1 cup white wine
3 cups vegetable broth
1 ½ tsp salt
1 tsp black pepper
1 TBS sugar
14.5 oz can of chopped tomatoes and juice

CONDIMENT: Italian crusty bread

DIRECTIONS:

1. Sauté onion and garlic in deep saucepan.
2. Add tomatoes and vegetable broth.
3. Add salt, pepper, and sugar.
4. Add white wine.
5. Simmer for 15 minutes.
6. Add fish and cook for 30-40 minutes, till fish is done.
7. Spoon into bowls.
8. Sprinkle with chopped parsley and serve with condiment.

SERVES 4-6

Sicilian Fish and Olives – Aunt Sara Falcone

INGREDIENTS:

2 lb fresh fish (tilapia, cod, or snapper)
1 large onion, chopped
¼ cup olive oil
3 fresh tomatoes, chopped or 1 can of chopped tomatoes
¼ cup sweet basil, chopped
1 leek, chopped thin
4 red potatoes cut in quarters
2 TBS capers
10 cracked green olives
Salt and pepper to taste

DIRECTIONS:

1. In a large deep skillet, sauté onions and leeks with olive oil.
2. Add tomatoes and basil simmer for 10 minutes.
3. Add the potatoes, capers, and green olives; simmer until potatoes are almost completely cooked.
4. Add fish, cook another 20 minutes.

SERVES 4-6

Marinated Fresh Dungeness Crab

Fresh Dungeness crab is always a treat for the holidays and more. I was taught this delight by Uncle Nunzio Alioto. This quickly became a family favorite passed down the generations. Living in California I pioneered this amazing dish to my family.

INGREDIENTS:

4-6 fresh whole crabs, boiled, cracked, and cleaned (you buy them this way)
8 whole cloves garlic, sliced thin
2 TBS Italian oregano
¾ cup extra virgin olive oil
½ cup balsamic vinegar
2 TBS cracked black pepper
1 tsp salt

DIRECTIONS:

1. In a large container with a tight seal, such as large Tupperware marinating container, place the crab.
2. Spread sliced garlic over crab.
3. Sprinkle cracked black pepper and salt over crab.
4. In olive oil, mix oregano and balsamic vinegar.
5. Pour olive oil mixture over crab.
6. Close tightly and shake container so all crab is coated.
7. Continue doing this every hour or so until ready to serve.
8. Place in large platter or bowl, have empty bowl nearby for shells.

SERVES 8-10

Sicilian Breaded Prawns

Marrietta's specialty, it was a Friday night treat.

INGREDIENTS:

16 giant prawns, peeled and deveined
1 ½ cups breadcrumbs
4 cloves of garlic, pressed
2 TBS parsley, chopped
1 tsp sea salt
½ tsp black pepper
¼ cup olive oil
1 TBS butter
2 eggs, beaten
1 cup of flour

DIRECTIONS:

1. In 3 separate bowls:
2. In bowl 1, place 1 cup of flour.
3. In bowl 2, place 2 beaten eggs.
4. In bowl 3, place breadcrumbs, garlic, parsley, salt and pepper.
5. Dip prawns in flour, then egg, then breadcrumbs ,and place on platter.
6. In a large skillet, mix olive oil and butter, have heat medium to medium-low.
7. Place prawns in heated skillet, turning once till golden brown.

SERVES 4-6

Note: Prawns cook quickly, do not over cook! Serve piping hot or as a cold hors d'oeuvre.

Spicy Shrimp Pizza

Note: Whole Foods and Trader Joe's have wonderful premade pizza dough for an easy pizza night.

INGREDIENTS:

1 cup coarsely grated provolone cheese
½ cup coarsely grated swiss cheese
2 cups small cooked shrimp
1/3 cup of green onions, chopped
½ tsp Italian oregano
½ tsp cracked black pepper
¼ tsp ground red pepper flakes

DIRECTIONS:

1. Heat oven to 425° and prepare crust as directed.
2. Roll out into pizza pan.
3. Add other ingredients starting with the cheese.
4. Bake 20 min and serve.

SERVES 4

Crab Supper Pie

INGREDIENTS:

1 cup of shredded Swiss cheese
1 unbaked 9-inch pastry shell
8 oz of flaked fresh crabmeat
2 green onions chopped, green part also
3 beaten eggs
1 cup of light cream
½ tsp salt
½ tsp grated lemon peel
¼ tsp dry mustard
¼ cup of sliced almonds (optional) or garlic flavored breadcrumbs

DIRECTIONS:

1. Sprinkle cheese on the bottom of shell, top with crabmeat.
2. Sprinkle with green onion.
3. Combine eggs, cream, salt, lemon peel, and dry mustard.
4. Pour over crabmeat.
5. Top with sliced almonds or garlic flavored breadcrumbs.
6. Bake 325° for 45 minutes or until set.
7. Remove from oven and let stand 10 minutes before serving.

SERVES 6

· Poultry ·

Marinated Chicken Wings Sicilian Style

JD's Beloved Sicilian Pasta, Chicken and Peas

Oven Fried Chicken

"Poultry"
And they fed the multitudes.

Marinated Chicken Breasts Sicilian Style

INGREDIENTS:

6 chicken breasts, washed and dried
6 cloves garlic, pressed
1 tsp salt
1 TBS cracked black pepper
½ cup of olive oil
1 TBS of dried Italian oregano
¼ cup balsamic vinegar

DIRECTIONS:

1. In a 9"x13" baking dish place chicken.
2. Sprinkle salt, pepper, and oregano both sides.
3. Add pressed garlic.
4. Add ½ cup olive oil over chicken.
5. Add balsamic vinegar.
6. Marinate 1-2 hours or night before.
7. Place chicken breast on broiler pan.
8. Cook 10 minutes each side, DO NOT OVERCOOK.
9. While chicken is cooking take marinate sauce.
10. Put in small saucepan and boil for 10 minutes.
11. Serve over broiled chicken.

SERVES 4-6

Note: Sweet basil and lemon juice can be substituted in place of oregano and vinegar. Both are delicious! This can also be broiled on your grill outdoors. I love this with wings.

Cornish Hens with White Grapes

INGREDIENTS:

4 small Cornish hens
Sea salt
Fresh cracked black pepper
1 bunch of seedless green grapes
8 stripes of pancetta (bacon can be substituted)
2 TBS extra virgin olive oil
1 oz of unsalted butter

DIRECTIONS:

1. Preheat oven to 425°
2. Season the washed and dried hens with coarse salt and pepper inside and out.
3. Place 3 or 4 grapes inside cavity of hens.
4. Wrap pancetta around the hen, tie with kitchen string. Also tie the legs together.
5. In 9"x 13" inch oblong casserole place the hens breast side up.
6. Drizzle with olive oil and butter.
7. Cook for 30-40 minutes until hens are golden brown.
8. Lower heat to 350° and continue cooking 30 more minutes until done.

SERVES 4

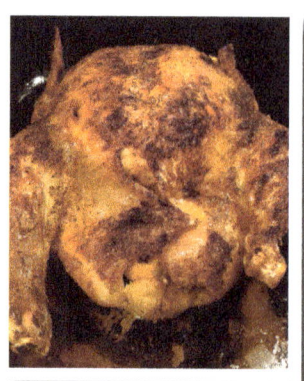

Oven Fried Chicken – Marrietta's

INGREDIENTS:

1 cut up fryer or packaged favorite parts
Salt
Pepper
Paprika
Garlic salt
1 cup of flour in plastic bag
2 TBS olive oil

DIRECTIONS:

1. Wash and dry chicken.
2. Season heavily with above ingredients, both sides.
3. This can be refrigerated up to a day before.
4. Remove chicken from refrigerator and placing 3-4 pieces in plastic bag with flour, shake until coated.
5. Line a cookie sheet with aluminum foil and rub olive oil on foil.
6. Shake chicken as you remove from the bag and place on cookie sheet.
7. Repeat until all chicken is floured.
8. Preheat oven to 375°.
9. Place cookie sheet in oven and turn chicken after cooking for 30 minutes on one side.
10. Remove put on platter, and enjoy healthy fried chicken.

SERVES 4-6

Note: This recipe can be doubled or tripled. Great for picnics!

JD's Beloved Sicilian Pasta, Chicken, and Peas

INGREDIENTS:

1 large roaster pan with lid
2 chickens cut up or packages of parts you like
2 large onions, chopped
2 large carrots, peeled and sliced thin
9-10 cloves of garlic, pressed
2 potatoes peeled and quartered, sliced thin
¾ cup of fresh Italian parsley, chopped
1 can of sweet peas with juice
½ bottle white wine (any brand)
1 TBS black pepper (or more)
3 TBS salt
1-2 lbs of pasta (depending on number of people)

CONDIMENTS: Grated cheese, red pepper flakes

DIRECTIONS:

1. Wash chicken and place in large roaster.
2. Season heavily with salt and pepper.
3. Add all ingredients except peas.
4. Place in oven at 500° uncovered turning once at about 25 minutes.
5. Cover. Reduce heat to 350°, cook 1 hour more.
6. Add peas and juice and continue to cook while pasta is cooking.
7. Remove chicken from roaster, place on platter.
8. Add drained pasta to roaster juice. (Keep 2 cups of salted pasta water to thin sauce if needed).
9. Place pasta on large platter, serve with condiments.

1 LB OF PASTA SERVES 6

Note: Sauce can be frozen with chicken for later.

Gina's Chicken Piccata

INGREDIENTS:

4 skinless and boneless chicken breast sliced thin
(1 chicken breast makes 2 thin slices)
1 (8 oz) jar of capers
¾ cup Sherry wine
2 lemons
Salt and pepper
4 TBS butter
4 TBS olive oil

DIRECTIONS:

1. Salt and pepper chicken both sides, then flour, shaking off excess flour.
2. In a large skillet with lid, brown chicken breast in 2 TBS olive oil and 2 TBS butter.
3. Remove breast and place on platter.
4. Add remaining butter and oil to skillet.
5. Zest the skins of 2 lemons, then cut in half and juice into skillet.
6. Add Sherry and stir.
7. Put chicken back into skillet.
8. Pour capers and juice onto chicken and simmer covered for 15 minutes.
9. Place on large platter and serve with juices.

SERVES 4-6

Marilyn's Hoisin Chicken

INGREDIENTS:

1 pkg 10-12 whole chicken wings or 1 whole chicken cut in pieces
3 TBS Hoisin sauce
3 TBS soy sauce
1 tsp granulated garlic
1 tsp ground ginger
2 dashed tabasco sauce
½ cup ketchup
3 heaping TBS brown sugar

DIRECTIONS:

1. Mix all ingredients together in a bowl and let stand while preparing chicken.
2. After washing and drying chicken, pour mixture over chicken in 9x13" casserole and marinate for at least 2-3 hours or overnight.
3. Bake at 350° uncovered until chicken is tender.

SERVES 4-6

Note: This was my Aunt Jo's favorite chicken that I made for her when she came to my house to visit. Wings were her favorite part of the chicken. Special memory of love between aunt and niece.

Gina's Chicken Piccata

Chicken Cacciatore – Marrietta's (Mom)

INGREDIENTS:

1 large roasting pan with lid
4 chickens, cut up or favorite parts
4 large onions, chopped
20 pieces or more of garlic (2 large bulbs) pressed
1 cup of fresh basil, chopped
½ cup of Italian parsley, chopped
2 TBS Italian oregano
3 TBS Salt
2 TBS pepper
2 cups red wine
2 packages sliced mushrooms

DIRECTIONS:

1. Add all of the chicken to roaster with all of the above ingredients except mushrooms.
2. Preheat oven to 450°.
3. Place open roaster in oven and sauté, keep turning so all is sautéed.
4. Reduce heat to 350°

SERVES 10-12

2 lbs of pasta for family gathering, less according to the number of people.
You will have sauce left over. Freeze in containers with chicken for quick and delicious dinners.

SAUCE FOR CACCIATORE

INGREDIENTS:

2 (6 oz) cans of tomato paste
4 (28 oz) cans of chopped tomatoes and juice
4 (28 oz) cans of water
6 TBS sugar
Salt to taste

DIRECTIONS:

1. Place tomato paste in 6 ½ quart size pan, dissolve with 4 or more (6oz) cans of water.
2. Add tomatoes with 4 (28oz) cans of water.
3. Stir, add sugar and salt.
4. Heat thoroughly for 30 minutes.

Marry the Sauce and the Chicken

DIRECTIONS:

1. Pour tomato sauce over browned chicken in roaster.
2. Add sliced mushrooms.
3. Combine tomato, chicken, and juices until all are blended.
4. Continue cooking covered at 350° for 1 hour or until chicken is done.
5. Remove chicken (Do not over cook).
6. Place on platter and set aside.
7. Leave sauce in oven to cook, uncovered, for 30-40 more minutes.
8. Last 15 minutes of cooking, cook pasta as directed.
9. Drain, place in platter, add sauce to cover pasta and serve with chicken on side.

MEMORIES OF CHICKEN CACCIATORE

A dish of love that has turned into tradition for our family. I loved Saturday when mom would prepare chicken cacciatore, to be cooked on Sunday morning. I was by her side and a good helper - peeling garlic, cleaning basil, chopping onions, slicing mushrooms. Dad would wash the chickens and cut them - it was a family affair!

The reward was waking up to the smell of everything cooking in the oven on Sunday morning- it was hard to leave the house for church but we knew what awaited us at Sunday dinner.

I hear the word and Sunday springs to mind. The day begins waking up to the smell of heavenly cacciatore cooking in the oven, its sauce bathing the chicken to tender perfection.

Looking back I'm firmly convinced our mothers used these Sunday dinners to move their families from sleeping to rising and getting dressed for church. Then happily hurrying off with the promise of enjoying the feast we would have when returning home. It always worked no matter how old we were and even after marriage — Sunday dinner at Mom and Dad's was a given.

It was the perfect time to catch up with each other after leaving the nest. It was tradition.

Have we lost those special times and memories in a world moving too fast and too cluttered with activities to savor the value of home and family? I wonder.

Apricot Glazed Hens – Marilyn's

This glaze is wonderful with pork chops or chicken, too!

INGREDIENTS:

6 Cornish hens, washed, drained, and patted dry
2 apples, peeled and chopped
1 large onion, chopped
1 stalk of celery, chopped small
½ cup cran raisins
1 tsp ginger
1 tsp curry powder
1 tsp garlic salt
1 tsp pepper
1 tsp coarse sea salt

Mix all above ingredients for stuffing the hens.

DIRECTIONS FOR STUFFING:

1. Stuff each hen tightly; skewer closed.
2. Rub hens lightly with coarse sea salt.
3. Place in large casserole and set aside.

INGREDIENTS FOR GLAZE:

2 cans apricot nectar
1 large can apricot halves, drained. Reserve juice.
3 TBS Worcestershire sauce
1 tsp cinnamon
2 heaping TBS honey
½ jar apricot jam or apricot pineapple jam

Mix all above ingredients together, except apricot halves and reserved juice.

DIRECTIONS:

1. Pour half of the glaze over the hens and cover.
2. Place in preheated 350° oven for 1 hour.
3. Remove from oven and take excess juice from pan with turkey baster.
4. Add remaining glaze and apricot halves over hens and cook uncovered 25-30 more minutes.

* Cook Uncle Ben's long grain and wild rice in apricot reserved juice and excess juice from Cornish hens.

A WHOLE HEN SERVES 6-8 ADULTS. IF CUT IN HALF, SERVES SMALLER EATERS.

Sicilian Breaded Chicken

This dish is wonderful with flank steak as well!

INGREDIENTS:

2-3 lbs. boneless, skinless chicken breast
1½ to 2 cups dry bread crumbs
5 cloves garlic, pressed
1 tsp salt
1 tsp pepper
¼ cup grated Romano cheese
¼ cup chopped parsley
2-3 eggs, beaten
½ cup flour
3 TBS olive oil

DIRECTIONS:

1. Butterfly chicken breasts, set aside.
2. In 3 shallow dishes, put flour in bowl 1, beat eggs in bowl 2, in bowl 3 mix bread crumbs, garlic, salt, pepper, cheese and parsley.
3. First dip chicken in flour, then egg, then breadcrumbs. Set on platter.
4. Heat 3 TBS olive oil in large skillet on medium heat. Place breaded meat in skillet, when red comes to top, turn and cook 5 to 7 minutes. Place on platter.

Wonderful with any pepper dish!

SERVES 4-6

Marrietta's Holiday Turkey

Always perfect, every time.

TURKEY INGREDIENTS:

1 16-20 lb tom turkey, washed and cleaned inside and out (remove giblets and cook separately)
1 TBS garlic salt
1 TBS poultry seasoning
1 TBS black pepper
1 TBS paprika
1 TBS sea salt
4 cubes butter

GRAVY INGREDIENTS:

1 qt jar
½ cup flour
warm water to fill jar to the top
1 pkg mini bella mushrooms

GRAVY

1. Place roaster with turkey juice on top of stove.
2. Turn stove on medium high heat and scrape the bottom of roaster of all bits and pieces.
3. Meanwhile, in a quart jar place ½ cup flour then fill the rest of the jar with warm water. Shake jar vigorously until the flour is totally dissolved and no lumps remain.
4. In bubbling turkey juice, slowly add flour and water mixture.
5. Juice will begin to thicken, adjust seasoning, and add 1 package of sliced mini bella mushrooms.
6. Cook until gravy is desired consistency.
7. Put in saucepan to keep warm on stove.

DIRECTIONS:

1. Mix all seasonings together, except for butter.
2. Rub seasonings generously inside and outside of turkey.
3. Turkey should be ice cold.
4. Stuff turkey with hamburger rice stuffing also ice cold. (See pg. 72 for stuffing)
5. Fill cavity and neck of turkey, keeping together with skewers and cooking string.
6. Place in large roasting pan, rub butter on top.
7. Cover and bake in over at 375° for 40 minutes.
8. Reduce heat to 325° and bake another 3 hours until turkey is done. Using a roasting thermometer it should read 175 when done.
9. Baste frequently as soon as juice is formed.
10. Remove turkey from roasting pain and let sit on a platter at least 30 minutes before carving.
11. Dressing can also be removed prior to carving.

SERVES 10-20

Hamburger

When I was a little girl I remember Sundays when my grandparents would come for dinner and a big pot of sugo (sauce) was cooking on the stove, bubbling in a perfect rhythm. Mom used to take a small bowl put a piece of bread on the bottom, cover it in sauce then plop a meatball on top. This was Sunday morning breakfast. I couldn't wait for the pasta, chicken feet, neck bones, sausage, that dinner would bring. Sundays were a glorious time in the kitchen and was always a family day. This was the tradition all through my youth and early married life, before life took us to different locations and away from my parents and grandparents.

Luckily a lot of our traditions were carried on with our new families and today I see my children carrying on for their children. These are the gifts that money cannot buy, they are the heart and soul of family and we wear our tradition like a badge of honor.

Meatballs – A must when making Sugo

You will have an abundance of sauce to freeze in containers, with enough meat for each meal. And of course the first meal, which you will enjoy that evening. This is a wonderful weekend venture to enjoy!

INGREDIENTS:

3lbs hamburger
6 eggs
1 cup of wet bread crumbs
6 cloves garlic, pressed
½ cup chopped parsley
½ cup grated asiago cheese
1 tsp salt
1 tsp pepper

DIRECTIONS

1. Mix all ingredients together in a glass bowl.
2. Form meatballs rolled in your hands to the size you desire.
3. Brown in skillet with a little oil on both sides.
4. When process is complete, add to the large pot and be careful not to break apart when stirring sauce.

Note: Each 1 lb of hamburger makes about 12-15 meatballs.

Cooking time is 2-3 hours until all meat is tender. Sauce is cooked always at a low simmer.

Hamburger and Rice Turkey Stuffing – Mom's

INGREDIENTS:

2 lb hamburger
5 cloves of garlic, pressed into hamburger when browning
1 ½ cup jasmine cooked rice
3 stalks celery, chopped
½ bunch Italian parsley, chopped
1 large onion, chopped
¼ cup olive oil
2 heaping tsp sage
Salt and pepper to taste

DIRECTIONS:

1. In large skillet, put olive oil, celery, parsley, onion, and sauté until tender.
2. Add salt, pepper, and sage.
3. In same skillet push aside sautéed mixture and add hamburger and garlic until no pink shows.
4. Mix everything together in skillet, adjust seasoning and set aside.
5. In cooked rice, add hamburger mixture and mix thoroughly.
6. Cool stuffing completely.

Note: Always remember if stuffing goes into the turkey it is cold stuffing to cold turkey. Stuffing can also be cooked separately in a casserole in the oven for 30-45 minutes at 350°.

SERVES 12-14

Annette's Hot Hamburger Sandwiches

My cousin made these for lunch one summer when I came home to visit. They have been apart of our family favorites ever since.

INGREDIENTS:

3 lbs lean ground beef
1 lb shredded cheddar cheese
1 (15 oz) can of tomato sauce
1 (6 oz) can ripe pitted olives chopped
I medium onion, chopped
3 tsp salt
1 ½ tsp garlic powder or granulated garlic
Freshly ground black pepper to taste
12 hoagie buns or 2 dozen French rolls

DIRECTIONS:

1. Brown the hamburger and cook completely.
2. Mix all other ingredients together and add the hamburger.
3. Cut off the tops of the rolls and scoop out the middle with fingers.
4. Save breadcrumbs for something else.
5. Fill the rolls with the meat mixture and wrap individual in foil.
6. Place on cookie sheet.

If unfrozen bake at 400° for 20 minutes.
If frozen bake at 400° for 45-60 minutes.

Note: These can be made ahead of time and freeze beautifully. Great for kids parties or Super Bowl Sunday.

Pastari

An Easter must-have.

THINGS NEEDED: Pasta machine

INGREDIENTS FOR DOUGH:

2 ½ lb flour
2 egg yolks (save whites)
1 cup Crisco
1 tsp salt
1 TBS sugar
2 cups cold water (maybe ½ more)
Note: Dough can be made in cuisinart with kneading parts.

DIRECTIONS FOR DOUGH:

1. When handling dough, lightly flour to keep from sticking.
2. Breaking dough in small parts, run each part through pasta machine up to #4.
3. Lay strip of dough on floured surface.
4. Cut with a 2lb coffee lid.
5. Fill with 1 heaping tablespoon of hamburger mixture.
6. Bring dough to center and flute all the way down to either side forming boat shape.
7. Using egg whites seal top of boats.
8. Bake on cookie sheet 350° for 20-25 minutes, until golden brown.

INGREDIENTS FOR MEAT FILLING:

10 lb hamburger, browned and drained
Place in a large bowl and:
2 bunches of fresh parsley, chopped
2 bulbs garlic, chopped
¼ cup sea salt
¼ cup coarse black pepper (more according to taste)
10 eggs at least to moisten mixture
2 cups of grated Romano cheese
Mix all-together, if mixture is too dry add 2 more eggs.

Note: These treats are traditionally cooked at Easter, but loved so much that Easter comes more than once a year. They can be frozen in freezer bags and popped out for use anytime.

MAKES APPROXIMATELY 125

 My cousin and I spend a whole day making these tasty meat boats for the whole family. Our mothers taught us well.

Nebraska Runzas

Runzas and Nebraska football go hand and hand. A Runza is yeast dough, filled with hamburger, cabbage, and baked.

INGREDIENTS FOR RUNZA DOUGH:

- 2 cups warm water
- 2 packages dry yeast
- ½ cup sugar
- 1 ½ tsp salt
- 1 egg
- ¼ cup butter (melted and cooled)
- 6 ½ cups flower

DIRECTIONS FOR RUNZA DOUGH:

1. Mix water, yeast, sugar and salt.
2. Stir till dissolved and add egg and butter.
3. Stir in flour and mix into dough.
4. Cover and place in the refrigerator for 4 hours.
5. Roll dough into oblong shape and cut into 16 squares.

INGREDIENTS FOR HAMBURGER FILLING:

- 1 ½ lb lean hamburger
- ½ cup onion, chopped
- 3 cups shredded cabbage
- ½ cup water
- 1 ½ tsp salt
- ½ tsp pepper
- Dash of Tabasco or more

DIRECTIONS FOR HAMBURGER FILLING:

1. Brown hamburger and onion, drain.
2. Add cabbage, seasoning, and water.
3. Simmer 15-20 minutes.
4. Cool completely before putting into dough.
5. Fill dough with hamburger mixture and press edges together.
6. Bake 20 minutes on a greased cookie sheet at 350°.

SERVES 10-12

✥ MEMORIES OF MAKING RUNZAS

My mother was one of the first cheerleaders at Nebraska University. She taught us all a great love for our Nebraska Cornhuskers. Go Huskers!

Marilyn's Shepherd's Pie

INGREDIENTS:

2 lbs lean hamburger
1 large onion, chopped
3 stalks of celery, chopped
¼ cup parsley, chopped
1 (14.5 oz) can whole kernel corn drained
6 large russet potatoes
½ cup milk
¾ stick of butter
1 heaping TBS sour cream
Paprika for garnish
½ tsp garlic salt
½ tsp black pepper
1 tsp salt

CONDIMENTS: Green salad, garlic bread

DIRECTIONS:

1. Brown the onion, celery, and parsley.
2. Add garlic salt and pepper.
3. Add ground beef to skillet.
4. Cook until no pink shows.
5. Add drained can of corn.
6. Simmer for 15 minutes.
7. While sautéing all of the above, in a separate pot peel and slice potatoes.
8. Add tsp of salt and cook until tender.
9. Drain potatoes, reserving ½ cup of the water.
10. Add butter, milk, and sour cream to potatoes.
11. Whip with electric beater till mashed potatoes are formed.
12. Taste and adjust salt.
13. In 9"x13" baking dish place hamburger ingredients on bottom.
14. Cover with mashed potatoes till no hamburger shows.
15. Sprinkle with paprika.
16. Place under broiler for 10-15 minutes and serve.

SERVES 6

 Cold winter days, a crisp fall breeze, maybe an extra long project at work or school. Nothing goes right — not the project or maybe just a conversation, pressure, tension, stress. The perfect time for Shepherd's Pie. Simple, yet consistently good. A whole meal in one.

Meat
Beef · Lamb · Veal · Pork

Roasting Sicilian Easter Lamb

Easter Tulips

Easter Brunch

"Beef"
Eat your steak and be strong like a lion.

"Lamb"
The meal of hope, because Easter was not Easter without lamb.

"Pork"
Something special and tasty.

Tournedo Strip – Ann Beck

INGREDIENTS:

5 lb tournedo strip (tenderloin)
2/3 stick butter
2 TBS Worcestershire sauce
1 TBS coarse black pepper
1 tsp of dry mustard
5 cloves of garlic, pressed

DIRECTIONS:

1. Place foil on bottom of roaster, then put strip on top.
2. Mix all ingredients together and pour over strip.
3. Bake at 350° for 35 minutes, DO NOT OVERCOOK!

MAKES 15-18 SLICES

Tri-Tip With Champagne Mushroom Sauce

INGREDIENTS:

1 (3 lb) tri-tip
¼ cup of Montreal steak seasoning or any favorite rub
1 lb sliced brown mushrooms
¼ cup of shallots, minced
2 cups champagne
2 TBS of Dijon mustard
7 oz sour cream
Salt and pepper to taste

DIRECTIONS:

1. Rub tri-tip with seasoning.
2. Baked in oven at 350° until rare in the middle (use your meat thermometer).
3. While meat is cooking, in skillet on the stove sauté shallots and mushroom until liquid is absorbed.
4. Add champagne and Dijon mustard.
5. Bring to a boil, reduce to half.
6. Reduce heat and add sour cream.
7. Salt and pepper to taste.
8. Place tri-tip on platter and add champagne mushroom sauce, serve.

SERVES 6-8

Italian Stew in Slow Cooker – Aunt Grace's

INGREDIENTS:

2 lbs stew meat (season with salt and pepper)
4 carrots, chopped
4 potatoes, quartered
2 stalks of celery, chopped
2 medium onions, quartered
4 cloves garlic, pressed
¼ tsp Italian oregano
¼ cup fresh basil, chopped
1 can cream of tomato soup
1 small can tomato sauce
½ cup red wine

DIRECTIONS:

1. Lay meat on bottom of cooker.
2. Layer with carrots, celery, onion, garlic, potatoes, oregano, and basil.
3. Add tomato soup, tomato sauce, and wine.
4. Cover and bake at 250° for 5-6 hours or until done.

SERVES 4-5

Sicilian Fausomauro (Braciole) – Nana Oddo's

INGREDIENTS:

2 lb of flank steak
1 large onion, sautéed
½ cup cooked rice
¼ cup breadcrumbs
¾ cup of parsley, chopped
¼ cup fresh basil, chopped
6 cloves garlic, pressed
1 cup grated cheese
4 eggs
1 lb hamburger

DIRECTIONS:

1. Mix all ingredients together, except flank steak, like meatballs.
2. Lay flank steak out individually.
3. Spread the above mixture on top of flank steak.
4. Roll together and tie with cooking string (should make 4 rolled fausomauro). Make sure the meat is tied so the ingredients do not fall out.
5. Sauté in olive oil, just until browned on both sides.
6. These treats finish cooking in your pot of sugo.
7. When removed from sauce, cut strings, and slice.
8. Place on platter, cover with sauce, and serve with pasta.

SERVES 6-8

Note: My Nana made hard boiled eggs and added sliced eggs to the roll.

Leg of Lamb or Lamb Shanks – Mom's Sicilian Style

INGREDIENTS:

1 large leg of lamb
4 large lamb shanks
20 cloves of garlic, chopped
1 cup fresh parsley, chopped
4 TBS sea salt
3 TBS black pepper

DIRECTIONS:

1. Mix garlic, parsley, salt, and pepper in small bowl.
2. Make slits in leg of lamb and stuff seasoning mixture into slits. Do the same if making lamb shanks.
3. Make as many slits as possible until all mixture is used.
4. Place leg of lamb in roaster uncovered at 350°
5. Use meat thermometer for medium rare.
6. Add 1 cup of red wine to drippings the last 30 minutes; baste for the remaining cooking time.

SERVES 8-10

Note: If making lamb shanks, cover during cooking time. Bake at 350° for approximately 1 hour to 1 hour and 15 minutes. Add wine the last 30 minutes of cooking time.

LAMB SHANKS SERVES 4

Leg of Lamb – Jackie's Napoli Style

INGREDIENTS:

1 large leg of lamb
1 cup of dry breadcrumbs, season with salt and pepper
3 wet bread slices added to the dry
10 cloves garlic, chopped
1 cup fresh mint, chopped
½ cup parsley, chopped
1 tsp red pepper flakes
5 lemons, juiced

DIRECTIONS:

1. Mix all above ingredients together in a bowl, except for lemon juice.
2. Make large slits in lamb, lots of them.
3. Stuff with filling, until all used.
4. Place leg of lamb in large roaster.
5. Start at 500° for 20-30 minutes uncovered until top of lamb becomes crusty.
6. Reduce heat to 325° and continue cooking in open roaster, basting frequently with the juice of the lemons.
7. Use meat thermometer to reach your desired rareness.

SERVES 8-10

Nana Oddo's Fava Beans and Pork Chops

"The food of the Gods" – Nana's Quote

INGREDIENTS:

2 pork chops center cut bone in
2 lbs fresh fava beans
1 (28 oz) can diced tomatoes
1 large onion, chopped
4 cloves of garlic, pressed
½ cup fresh basil, chopped
1 TBS sugar
Garlic salt, salt, and pepper to taste

DIRECTIONS:

1. Season pork chops with salt, pepper, and garlic salt.
2. Brown on both sides in large skillet then set aside on platter.
3. In the same skillet sauté onion, garlic, basil, until onions are soft.
4. Add can of tomatoes, sugar, salt, pepper, and cook 10 minutes.
5. Add clean and shucked fava beans and pork chops.
6. Cover and cook until chops are tender and favas are cooked; 30-40 minutes depending on how thin chops are.

SERVES 2

Sicilian Baby Back Ribs

INGREDIENTS:

1 slab baby back ribs
½ cup balsamic vinegar
¼ cup olive oil
1 tsp crushed Italian oregano
3 twists of cracked black pepper
1 TBS sea slat
4 cloves garlic, pressed

DIRECTIONS:

1. In a bowl, mix all ingredients together.
2. Place baby back ribs in a large Ziploc bag.
3. Pour ingredients into bag and seal.
4. Make sure the ribs are coated, keep turning during the marinating process.

This can be done up to a day ahead of time.

I cook a slab of ribs in my oven under the broiler:

1. Remove ribs from bag and reserve the juice and place in small saucepan.
2. While ribs are cooking, bring marinade to a boil and cook for 5-6 minutes.
3. Place ribs on cookie sheet and put in oven one rack above middle.
4. Broil for 15 minuets, turn over, and broil another 15 minutes on other side.
5. Remove from oven and cut ribs, place on platter.
6. Pour juice over ribs and serve.

Marilyn's Osso Buco

Served with a thin pasta or rice, mashed potatoes are good too!

INGREDIENTS:

8 pieces of veal shanks (about 6 ½ lbs)
5 TBS butter
2 carrots, peeled and diced
2 celery stalks, chopped
3 cloves of garlic, chopped
¾ cups flower
2 TBS olive oil
1 cup of wine red or white
1 (15 oz) can crushed tomatoes in puree
1 ½ cup chicken or beef stock broth
1 tsp dried basil
½ tsp rosemary
¼ tsp thyme
1 bay leaf
Salt and pepper to taste

GARNISH:

4 cloves of garlic, pressed
6 TBS parsley, chopped
2 tsp of grated lemon peel
1 can of anchovies, chopped
2 TBS olive oil

 My mom and dad loved this dish; it's the marrow that hooks everyone! Oh yes, and the garnish.

DIRECTIONS:

1. In a large Dutch oven, put butter in the pan. Add carrots, celery, onion, and garlic sauté just until onions start to color (7-8 min).
2. Season veal with salt and pepper, flour them.
3. Brown in skillet, turning on all sides.
4. Remove shanks.
5. Add wine to same skillet, add tomatoes stir in broth and spices.
6. Arrange shanks on top of vegetables in the Dutch oven.
7. Pour tomato wine mixture over shanks, bring to a boil. Cover and reduce heat to a low simmer for 1 ½ - 2 hours.
8. Serve in a deep-dish platter with the garnish on the side.

SERVES 6-8

special words

My mother taught us these beautiful words along with our first books ever read to us. No fairy tales in these words:

"Gilded walls and marbled floors can never make a home but any place where love abides and friendship is a gift, is surely home, and home sweet home, for there the heart can rest."

Remembering my family moments, there are certain times that stand out more than others. Mom and I enjoyed our moments in the kitchen together. It was a time to talk about everything my life, her life, every secret, thought, and dream. How lucky I was to have these special times with my mother and mentor. While my mother created and prepared our family meal, she was teaching and molding me into the Marilyn I am today. It was fun to sing an Opera verse talking and responding to one another. My younger brothers loved these almost nightly rituals, so much so, that as the years passed and I left for college, the adjustment was hardest for them. Oh the beauty of family, hard work, deep learning, and lots of laughter. We were so blessed with my mother's talent to ease emotions with the magic of her meals.

I remember the heavy labored footsteps of my father coming up the stairs after a long and draining day of a doctor's life. When you're young you only know that your dad is gone most of the time, 2 or 3 nights not home for dinner. The phone rang constantly and it wasn't for my brothers or me, most of the time. Luckily my mom kept us informed and we knew what my father did for others and what he sacrificed for all of our family.

Thus I grew up with a great respect for my father and tried never to take for granted what we all had because of his labors.

Mom's gift of love was the meal she prepared for him every day. His happiness was sharing it with all of us, talking and listening to our chatter around the table.

When I got old enough to understand, I realized that certain meals were prepared when my dad had especially trying times and days. Such a smart woman, my mentor, my mother.

I also remember the comfort of lying in bed, seeing the light down the hall, peeking from Mom and Dad's room, hearing

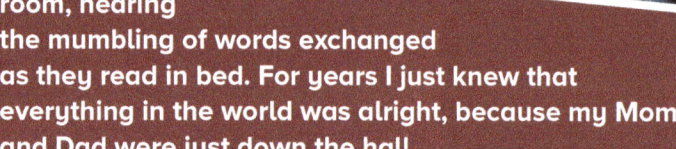

the mumbling of words exchanged as they read in bed. For years I just knew that everything in the world was alright, because my Mom and Dad were just down the hall.

These memories comforted me, along with the amazing meals my Mother created each and everyday for all of us.

If I said every memory was happy and joyful, it would bring a smile to many of our faces. I grew up and lived in a normal real family with yelling and fights. We are Sicilian after all, and sometimes not only do our hands work overtime; but so do our mouths. I believe living in reality is also a very important lesson in handling life, when we are exposed to life outside our protected home.

I learned that love of each other heals all wounds. Family is everything! No matter what happened, we always knew my Mom and Dad loved each other and all of us beyond words, and they did everything to protect our family. I am proud of my family and the humanness of us all.

Specialty Dishes

Uncle Sam's Italian Sausage

Pizza with Mushrooms

Watermelon Pickles - Grandma Runnel's

"Specialty Dishes"
These dishes are pure tradition.

Liathina (Head Cheese)

Mrs. Monaco was my Aunt Louise's mother-in-law and the queen of this delicacy. This was a special treat during holidays and special occasions!

INGREDIENTS:

3 lb pig ears (snout, tails, and hocks)
2 lb soup meat or chuck roast
4 lemons
1/3 cup white vinegar
Salt to taste
1 tsp red pepper flakes, or more if desired

DIRECTIONS:

1. Boil ears, snout, tails, and hocks, in water just to cover, and enough salt to taste in the water.
2. Boil meat in separate pot, water to cover, and enough salt to taste.
3. When meats are cooked, remove from water, and no do not throw out water.
4. Cut meat into small pieces.
5. Cut ears, hocks, tails, in pieces also after removing from water.
6. Place meat and ears in two 9"x13" casseroles.
7. Mix the juice of lemons and vinegar in 1 cup of pork water and 1 cup of beef water. Should make at least 3 cups of liquid.
8. Add red pepper flakes.
9. Pour over cut up meats, just enough to cover the top of the pieces.
10. Cover with plastic wrap and refrigerate until it congeals.
11. Cut in squares and serve.

SERVES 12-14

Uncle Sam's Italian Sausage

We do not make this in small quantity. The family experience is cherished by all. We gather all families together and make sausage for everyone!

INGREDIENTS:

30 lbs Boston pork butts = 25 lbs sausage (cut pork butts into chunks, removing excess fat)
Casing (31/32) - casing approximately 2 ½ feet long makes 1 ½ lb sausage
1 meat grinder
Scale needed to weigh meat according to what everyone wants

SEASONING FOR EVERY 4 LBS OF MEAT:

1. 1 oz salt
2. ½ oz black pepper (restaurant/rough black)
3. ¼ oz granulated garlic
4. ½ tsp ground anise
5. 1 tsp ground fennel
6. 1 tsp whole fennel
7. ¼ oz red pepper flakes
8. 1 tsp paprika
9. 1 cup water as needed to mix the meat

DIRECTIONS:

In a large mixing container put all spices and coat meat; easier to do in 4 lb increments.
Meat is put through the grinder and directly into the casing.

My Uncle Sam bought the whole fennel and ground fennel from the Franciscan Butcher Supply Company on 13th and Jackson, Omaha Nebraska.

Pickled Hot Banana Peppers

THINGS NEEDED:

Quart sized jars and lids
A dozen jars for a bushel of peppers

INGREDIENTS:

1 bushel banana peppers
2 heaping TBS sugar per jar
2 heaping TBS salt per jar
1 tsp pickling spice per jar
3-4 chunks of peeled garlic per jar
1 gallon white vinegar
1 gallon water

DIRECTIONS:

1. Wash peppers.
2. Cut stem top off of peppers and scoop out some of the seeds.
3. Put peppers one by one in the jars standing up, do not pack to tight.
4. Add salt, sugar, garlic, and pickling spice to each jar.
5. In a 2-gallon container mix vinegar and water equal parts making 2 gallons.
6. Pour over peppers in jar filling to the top.
7. Place lids on top, tighten, and shake until sugar and salt dissolve.
8. On large tray placed jars upside down over night.
9. Next day turn jars right side up.
10. Store in a cool place and takes at least 4 weeks before ready.
11. After opening, refrigerate.

1 JAR SERVES 6-8

Watermelon Pickles – Grandma Runnel's

INGREDIENTS:

1 watermelon (cut off green skin and all pink meat left on rind, cut in cubes or slices)

DIRECTIONS FOR PREPARING RIND:

1. Soak in 3 qt water and ½ cup salt overnight
2. Rinse and put rind in water and bring to a boil on the stove.
3. Immediately pour off water and set rind aside.

SYRUP INGREDIENTS:

In the same pot boil:
1½ cups water
3 cups cider vinegar
6 cups sugar
3 TBS whole all spice
3 TBS whole cloves
5 sticks of cinnamon (about 3 inches long)
Peel of 1 lemon sliced thin
Add the rinds when sugar is melted

DIRECTIONS:

1. Boil the rind and spices until the rind is transparent
2. Put in sterilized jars with some juice and spices.
3. The longer they stay in jars the better they are.

1 JAR SERVES 8-10

About Olive Oil

NEW THOUGHT

Finding the right olive oil is very important to me. It has to be full bodied and have a good taste; it is the wine of Italian cooking. My Nano would buy cases of extra virgin olive oil from a small community in California and have it shipped to the Midwest- that's how important it was to our cooking.

Olives are served with almost every meal. We learned to cure them, and I can't imagine giving up the task. Once you're hooked on the curing, your creativity kicks in — what type, what flavor, black or green.

There isn't an olive tree that is passed by without great attention and respect given to it. We also check to see if it has been harvested and if not, are the olives available for the picking?

I recall a holiday spent in Arizona at my oldest nephews home. He has 5 acres of land and his home is surrounded by olive trees. We were thrilled, he had never picked them. His years had been spent in school becoming a top-notch orthopedic surgeon. He was amazed that my husband emptied our suitcases and filled them with olives for our return trip to California. Our clothes went into tote bags carried on the plane. Needles to say my nephew is hooked, he now creates some of the tastiest olives in the family and rightfully calls them black gold.

All my brothers are good cooks. They learned from my Nano how to garden, make wine, vinegar, and cure olives.

Nano Oddo ordered direct from Ditomaso Olives in California. That's how important olive oil was to cooking.

Curing Black Olives

THINGS NEEDED:

1 large bucket
2 lb bag rock salt
5 lb black olives, uncured

DIRECTIONS:

1. Rinse olives and place in bucket.
2. Add rock salt to coat .
3. After 1-2 days, water will form in bucket.
4. Drain and continue to drain as water continues to form.
5. This process goes for at least 8-10 days.
6. More salt can be added if all dissolves.
7. Olives with become wrinkled.
8. Taste in 10 days to see if they are cured.
9. Put in jars with olive oil, they last for months.

Note: You can also add hot pepper flakes and dried oregano to your olives when serving. These olives are wonderful for cooking and eating. They are dryer and a little more salty than the calamata olive. My favorite of the blacks.

Curing Green Olives

THINGS NEEDED:
1 case quart jars and lids

INGREDIENTS:

3 lbs green olives (large or small)
2 TBS salt (per jar)
1 large whole clove garlic, peeled

DIRECTIONS:

1. Put salt in jar, add washed olives.
2. Add cold water to the top, place 1 garlic clove or 2 on top.
3. Seal with the lid tightly.
4. Shake jar to dissolve salt.
5. Repeat 2-3 times first day.
6. Place on shelf in cool place for 1 year.

Note: When you open a jar after the 10-12 months, jars may fizzle. This is normal, olives are delicious and not spoiled. After opening keep in refrigerator. I love them right out of the jar with that hint of garlic flavor. It completes any sandwich or cheese snack.
1. Olives can be drained and marinated in olive oil, chopped parsley, red pepper flakes for another variation.
2. Use your imagination and season your olives with different spices and chopped peppers etc.

Italian Cracked Olives – Nano's

INGREDIENTS:

1 lb cracked green olives
¼ cup red wine vinegar
¼ cup olive oil
3 stalks fresh cardooni or 3 stalks fresh celery
1 bunch fresh mint
1 tsp red pepper flakes
10 cloves garlic, sliced

DIRECTIONS:

1. In olive oil, sauté garlic, celery, and mint.
2. Add olives when celery is tender.
3. Add vinegar and let simmer.
4. When flavors have married removed from pan.
5. Can be stored in jars in the refrigerator up to 3 months.

Note: If you are lucky to find cardooni, preparation is as follows:
1. Cut into pieces and boil in salted water until tender.
2. Drain thoroughly and follow the steps above.

SERVES 15-20

Aunt Jo's Pizza Dough

I always make my pizza and cuddiruni so I can freeze some. They make great meals with a salad.

INGREDIENTS:

5 lbs of flour
3 TBS salt
1 heaping cup shortening
3 pkgs yeast
4 ¾ cup warm water
Olive oil (any amount)

DIRECTIONS FOR DOUGH:

1. Dissolve yeast in warm water before adding to flour.
2. Knead together all ingredients, add olive oil.
3. Knead until everything is together and smooth.
4. Put a little oil on top and spread around dough.
5. Put a clean cloth on top so dough is covered.
6. Let rise 1 hour for pizza.

Recipe can be cut in half, if you so choose.

MAKES 5 PIZZAS. Dough weighs 2 lbs per pizza. For double-crusted pizza weigh dough to 1 ½ lb, makes 4 double crusted pizzas.

SAUCE FOR PIZZA INGREDIENTS:

3 (28oz) cans of crushed tomatoes
6 large cloves of garlic, pressed
2 TBS sugar
Salt and pepper to taste
¼ cup of basil, chopped
1 tsp dried or fresh Italian oregano

Cook in skillet on stove for 30-35 minutes on low, until sauce has thickened.

TOPPINGS FOR PIZZA:

4 or 5 large onions chopped finely in processor
1 cup grated Parmesan Romano cheese
You can add topping to your pizzas, like cooked cauliflower, eggplant, mushrooms, and anchovies.

DIRECTIONS:

1. Roll out pizza dough to fit pizza pans.
2. Place a nice amount of sauce on top.
3. Add onions and cheese last.
4. Bake at 350° for 30 minutes.

FILLING FOR DOUBLE CRUSTED PIZZA (CUDDIRUNI*)

*Pronunciation depending on who said it:

1lb browned hamburger or sausage
1 bunch cooked Swiss chard drained well
1-2 thin sliced potatoes keep in cold water until ready to use
1 bunch steamed cauliflower or broccoli
½ cup of grated Romano cheese

Whatever ingredients you choose, mix with pizza sauce and some of the onion. Only the potatoes are laid flat on bottom of dough. Spread on bottom layer of dough, add cheese, place top layer of dough, and pinch all sides together like fluting a pie crust. Put olive oil on hand and rub on top of dough. Prick top of dough with fork. Bake at 350° for 30-45 minutes.

Note: If freezing pizzas, cook 10 minutes less to allow for time to heat in the oven.

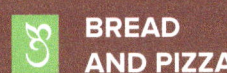

BREAD AND PIZZA

A time to join in and get those small hands accustomed to the feel of the art of cooking. Flour from head to toe, feeling important and needed and oh so accomplished! A lesson everyone can learn.

I learned that the simple touch of your hands could create great things. Every Friday pizza and bread was made. So I guess the "Famous Friday Pizza Day", has been around a long time, could our family tradition have been responsible for this? Wow!

Sicilian Tripe – 2 Ways

**Merry Christmas and Happy New Year.
We are Sicilians, a true Christmas tradition.**

INGREDIENTS FOR RED TRIPE SAUCE:

10 lbs honeycomb tripe*
1 large onion, chopped
6 cloves of garlic, pressed
1 (28 oz) can of crushed tomatoes in purée
1 large TBS sugar
1 ½ TBS pickling spice
1 tsp salt
1 tsp pepper

INGREDIENTS FOR WHITE TRIPE SAUCE:

10 cloves garlic, chopped
½ cup parsley, chopped
1 TBS red pepper flakes
½ cup olive oil
Juice from 6 lemons

TRIPE DIRECTIONS:

1. Cook tripe in boiling salted water until fork slides in and out easily.
2. Drain in colander, let cool.
3. After tripe as cooled, cut into 1"x1" inch pieces.
4. Set cooked trip aside.

RED SAUCE DIRECTIONS:

1. In skillet, sauté onion and crushed garlic with olive oil.
2. Add can of crushed tomatoes in purée.
3. Add sugar, salt, pepper, and pickling spice.
4. Let sauce cook and thicken.
5. In deep casserole, place 5 lbs of cooked and cut tripe.
6. Pour sauce over tripe, stirring to coat it all.
7. Cover and baked at 350° for 45 minutes.

WHITE SAUCE DIRECTIONS:

1. In skillet, sauté garlic, parsley, olive oil.
2. Add 5 lbs of cooked and cut tripe.
3. Add pepper flakes, continue to sauté for 10-15 minutes.
4. Add lemon juice.
5. Sauté another 5 minutes.
6. Remove from skillet, to serving dish.
7. Enjoy!

SERVES 10-12

*Note: I order tripe from the meat department at Safeway, always perfect. Mexican stores also carry honeycomb tripe, as do oriental stores.

Desserts

"Cannoli"
A meal's sweet reward.

"Saluté"
The Bakers of the Family

"Apricot Pie"
Just because you can.

Gnoccholi – Nana Oddo's Creation

DOUGH INGREDIENTS:

5 cups of flour
¾ cup of sugar
½ cup Crisco shortening
½ cup milk
4 heaping tsp baking powder
1 heaping tsp cinnamon
4 eggs

Can be stored in tins for 2-3 months, if they last that long.

HONEY MIXTURE INGREDIENTS PER BATCH

(2 cups of cooked gnoccholi):
½ cup of honey
1 tsp of cinnamon (add last)

DIRECTIONS:

1. In mixer, beat sugar, eggs, and shortening.
2. Add baking powder to flour. Slowly add to sugar, eggs, and shortening, alternating flour and milk. Add cinnamon last. Dough will form.
3. Taking small piece of dough, roll into a rope. Cut small pieces and place on cookie sheet.
4. Bake at 350° until light brown (15-20 min).
5. Cool completely.

MAKES 8 CUPS

DIRECTIONS FOR HONEY MIXTURE:

1. In a pan heat honey and cinnamon until brown.
2. In separate batches continue making honey mixture to coat each 2c batch of cooked gnoccholi.
3. On a large cutting board greased with butter, place each batch of honeyed gnoccholi.
4. Using hands form edible sized clusters.
5. Place on wax papered trays and let dry completely, until honey is no longer sticky.

Peach or Blackberry Cobbler

INGREDIENTS:

1 cup of sugar
1 cup of flour
1 cup of milk
1 tsp baking powder
1 pinch of salt
1 stick of butter
8-10 fresh peaches or 2 lbs fresh blackberries (who says you can't mix them together, cutting down quantity of course)

CONDIMENTS:

Heavy whipping cream
Ice cream
Heated juice of the fruit

DIRECTIONS:

1. Peel and slice the peaches cook about 5 minutes until reach a rolling boil. Add no water.
2. Add sugar and cinnamon to taste. Drain and save the juice.
3. Melt butter in 9"x13" baking dish, set aside to cool.
4. Mix the remaining ingredients and pour gently over melted butter.
5. Place fruit on top and bake at 350° for 35 minutes.
6. Can serve with 1 or all of the condiments.

SERVES 10-12

Marrietta's Apple Pie

INGREDIENTS FOR CRUST:

⅔ cup of shortening
2 cup of flour
½ tsp salt
¼ cup cold water
Mix all together to make dough. Wrap in plastic wrap and place in refrigerator for 30 minutes.

INGREDIENTS FOR PIE FILLING:

5 heaping cups of apples, peeled and cored
5 heaping TBS flour
¾ cup sugar
¼ cup brown sugar
1 ½ heaping tsp cinnamon
1 ½ tsp nutmeg
2 tsp lemon juice or more
Mix everything together in a bowl.

DIRECTIONS:

1. Remove pie crust from refrigerator cut in half. Roll out one half for bottom of pie.
2. Place crust in pie tin and poke with fork a few times.
3. Pour ingredients onto crust.
4. Roll second half of crust and place on top.
5. Flute and cut edges to fit pie tin.
6. Poke with fork several times on top.
7. Place pie in middle of oven on cookie sheet.
8. Bake at 350° for 55 minutes.

Note: I rub the top of the pie with TBS of milk and sprinkle with cinnamon and sugar. Gives a pretty glaze and beautiful color.

Apricot Pie
Nana Miloni's perfected by Marlene

INGREDIENTS:

4 cups apricots
1 ½ cup sugar (¾ brown and ¾ white)
2 TBS minute tapioca
2 TBS cornstarch
Juice of a lemon
¼ tsp cinnamon
¼ tsp nutmeg
3 TBS butter cubed
1 egg slightly beaten

Refer to Marrietta's Apple Pie for homemade pie crust.

DIRECTIONS:

1. Slice apricots and put them in a bowl.
2. In that same bowl, squeeze juice of lemon.
3. Add cinnamon, and let sit for 5-10 minutes.
4. In a separate bowl, add sugar, cornstarch, tapioca, and nutmeg.
5. Carefully mix the ingredients to blend well.

Easy method: Buy two 9" pie crusts ready made in grocery store.

1. Follow instructions and bring crust to room temp.
2. Place one 9" rolled out crust on bottom of 9" pie plate. Then add the apricot mixture.
3. Cut the butter into small cubes and place on top of the apricot mixture.
4. Add the top crust, cut and flute. Cut slits on top. Brush with egg wash and sprinkle with sugar.
5. Preheat oven to 450°
6. Place pie in middle rack; cook for 15-20 min.
7. Reduce heat to 375° and bake for 40 minuets.
8. If the crust is golden and the pie is bubbling, it is time to take it out.

Tip: Always cook pie on top of cookie sheet. Every oven is different so watch closely.

Apple Crisp

Aunt Marie Garro, my dad's baby sister.

INGREDIENTS:

12 or more apples peeled and cored
²/₃ cup of butter (cut into dry ingredients)
1 cup of brown sugar
¾ cup oatmeal
¾ cup flour
2 tsp cinnamon
2 tsp nutmeg

DIRECTIONS:

1. Mix everything together except apples.
2. In a large greased 9"x 13" baking dish place apples.
3. Pour mixed ingredients over apples.
4. Bake at 375° for 45-60 minutes.

SERVES 10-12

Devils Food Mayonnaise Cake – Aunt Jo's

INGREDIENTS:

2 cups flour, sifted
1 cup of sugar
4 TBS cocoa (bakers instant cocoa recommended)
2 tsp baking soda
1 cup of mayonnaise
¼ tsp salt
1 tsp vanilla
1 cup of cold water

DIRECTIONS:

1. Sift all dry ingredients together.
2. Mix mayonnaise, vanilla, and cold water together.
3. Add to dry ingredients and mix until well blended.
4. Grease and flour oblong cake pan.
5. Pour cake batter into pan.
6. Bake at 350° for 35-40 minutes. Always test cake to make sure toothpick comes out clean.

Note: Powdered sugar on cooled cake is a great topping. I made cupcakes with this moist and delicious recipe. Be creative!

SERVES 12-15 • MAKES 2 DOZEN CUPCAKES

Zabaione

Cousin Sam's from Salvatore's

INGREDIENTS:

5 egg yolks
3 ½ oz of super fine sugar
²/₃ cup of Marsala wine or sweet Sherry
Fragola – translated strawberries
Amaretti cookies

DIRECTIONS:

1. Whisk egg yolks and sugar until thick and doubled in volume.
2. Place over double boiler with water below, bring water to boil.
3. Add Marsala, keep whisking until it is warm (about 10 minutes).
4. Pour in wine glasses or bowl and serve surrounded with fragola and amaretti.

SERVES 4

My cousin Sam was loved and respected as an amazing chef, filled with wit and talent. His warmth was infectious to all who knew him. He taught me some of his skills. I am forever grateful.

Christmas Fruitcake
This is a delicious and rich treat!

Good all year 'round! A special gift from Aunt Francis Parrillo. East coast Italians, dear friends forever.

INGREDIENTS:

1 lb of dates • 1 lb of walnuts • 1 lb pecans
½ lb coconut
8 oz candied cherries (sliced)
8 oz candied pineapple (sliced)
1 can Eagle Brand milk
2 jiggers rum

DIRECTIONS:

1. Cut all fruit and mix nuts.
2. Add coconut, mix thoroughly.
3. Add Eagle Brand milk.
4. Continue to mix until everything is coated.
5. Place in angel food cake pan.
6. Preheat oven to 250°, place pan in oven center.
7. Bake for 2 hours; remove and let cool on rack.

FINAL DIRECTIONS FOR FRUITCAKE:

1. Put round piece of tin foil on bottom of cake pan.
2. Remove cake from pan; place in tin on top of foil.
3. Pour 1 jigger of rum all around the cake.
4. Cover with round foil on top of cake and place lid on tin. Refrigerate.
5. After 1 week, add 1 more jigger of rum and continue to refrigerate until ready to use.

The trick to fruitcake is letting the rum absorb for a 2-week period. If anxious, go for it after a week. Store fruitcake in the fridge in a covered round tin.

1 slice of fruitcake can be cut in fours and served.

Nana Oddo's Gnoccholi

Vacations and holidays are such a special time for families.

Marrietta's Famous Cheesecake

Given to her from the famous Lindy's New York Cheesecake.

INGREDIENTS FOR CHEESECAKE FILLING:

4 (3 oz) packages Philadelphia cream cheese
2 eggs
½ cup of sugar
1 (8oz) carton sour cream (add last)
½ tsp vanilla
Dash cinnamon
Note: Make crust first.

INGREDIENTS FOR GRAHAM CRACKER CRUST:

2 cups graham cracker crumbs (can be bought in box)
1 stick of butter
¼ cup sugar
¼ tsp cinnamon

DIRECTIONS:

1. Mix graham cracker crumbs, butter, sugar, and cinnamon together and pour into cheesecake pan. Spreading and padding it down with spoon moving up ¼ inch on side of the pan.
2. Put in freezer for 20-30 minutes while preparing the cheesecake filling.
3. Beat eggs and sugar in mix master.
4. Add cheese a little at a time, blend well.
5. Add sour cream, vanilla, and dash of cinnamon.
6. Remove crust from freezer.
7. Pour cheesecake filling into crust.
8. On center rack, place in oven at 400° for 25-30 minutes.
9. Cheesecake is done when toothpick comes out clean. Time may vary with ovens.

SERVES 10-12

Topping: be creative! Fresh fruit, strawberries, blueberries, or Comstock cherries in cans. (This was tradition while I was growing up).

Sfingi

Memories come alive on Christmas Eve standing around the stove waiting for the hot sfingi. A tradition everyone remembers.

INGREDIENTS:

1 large round glass bowl
3 cups flour
1 tsp salt
1 ½ TBS Crisco shortening (I knew it as spry)
2 cups warm water
1 package of Fleischmann's active dry yeast
1 egg
1 ½ TBS sugar
1 gallon of peanut oil
1 lb honey
Powdered sugar

DIRECTIONS:

1. Place flour in deep bowl, add salt and sugar, mix with hands.
2. Cut in Crisco.
3. Make hole in center of flour, slightly beat egg and put in center.
4. In measuring cup, put two cups warm water, add yeast and mix together till dissolved. Water must be warm.
5. Slowly add water and yeast to bowl, using both hands and quickly mixing all.
6. Cover bowl with heavy towel (beach towel) and place in a warm spot.
7. Let rise all day.
8. I use a 4-quart pan filled 3/4ths full with peanut oil on stove. This pan has been used since my Nana first started making sfeengee for us.
9. Spoon 1 TBS of dough into preheated hot oil, dough will rise to the top forming funny shaped balls.
10. Let cook until center of ball is no longer doughy (test a couple for timing). This takes a little time, but is worth it. My pan cooks 4-5 at a time. That is manageable. Remove from oil with slotted spoon.
11. In separate small pan heat half of honey with dash of cinnamon. As sfingi come out of oil, put in honey pot and coat.
12. Remove to a plate and serve right away.

Note: Do not wait for all sfingi to be done. Serve as they come out of the pot.
Option: powdered sugar can be sprinkled on sfingi instead of honey.

 "A REASON TO STAY AWAKE"
Italian version of doughnuts. Nana Oddo's recipe. Traditionally served on Christmas Eve, either before midnight mass or after. It wouldn't be Christmas without this amazing delight!

SERVES 20-25

Cannoli

Making cannoli was a great venture. My Nana, Mom, and Aunt would gather together with my cousin Geri and I under their feet, making these treats for the holidays. Always ahead of time! Later Geri and I brought our daughters into the mix, creating what our mothers and Nana had taught us.

NEEDED:

Cannoli tubes, deep fryer, pasta machine

INGREDIENTS:

5 cups flour
2 heaping TBS Crisco
5 TBS sugar
1 tsp salt
5 egg yolks (reserve the whites for later use)
¼ cup white wine
1 ⅛ cup cold water
1 large can of Crisco (goes into deep fryer to cook the shells in)

CANNOLI FILLING INGREDIENTS:

1 lb ricotta
½ cup sugar
½ cup candied cherries, chopped
½ cup dark chocolate, chopped
1 tsp rum extract (can use vanilla if desired)
Mix everything together.

DIRECTIONS:

1. When filling, use long teaspoon and make sure you fill to the center on side before turning to fill the other side.
2. Place on dish, sprinkle w/ powdered sugar.

Note: Chocolate or vanilla pudding can also be used to fill cannoli. If using packaged pudding always cut the liquid in half so pudding is thick. You can add chopped walnuts, crushed pineapple drained to a pulp, candied cherries, and chocolate chips.

DIRECTIONS:

1. Mix yolk, wine, and water together.
2. Add to flour, sugar, salt, and Crisco.
3. Mix thoroughly to form dough.
4. Prepare lightly floured large surface for dough after it is run through the pasta machine.
5. Starting at number 1 on pasta machine taking small portion of dough keep running through up to number 5. Dough will be right thinness after that.
6. Place strip on prepared surface.
7. Using the cannoli shells, cut dough to fit on shell. Not tightly, or dough will not come off of shell after cooked.
8. Seal dough together by rubbing egg whites with fingers on one side of dough and placing other flap on top.
9. Slowly place cannoli in hot deep fryer. Cannoli shell will turn light brown when cooked.
10. Remove and place on large surface to cool.
11. When cool slowly slide pastry shell from tube.
12. Shells can be stored in large airtight tins in a cool place until ready to use.

Note: Thus this can be made way ahead as it takes time and work for this delicacy.

ONE BATCH MAKES 75

Giugiulena

Giugiulena or Sheeshelena depending on who is speaking! The recipe is the original recipe from my Nana Oddo, perfected by Marilyn Longo!

INGREDIENTS:

1 lb giugiulena (two 8 oz jars, roasted white sesame seeds at Fry's or Whole Foods)
3 cups chopped almonds (shelled, not roasted or salted, medium chop in food processor)
½ lb honey (8oz)
1 ¾ cup of sugar
1 TBS butter

NOTE: ONLY MAKE 1 BATCH AT A TIME

DIRECTIONS:

1. In stainless steel medium-sized pan, cook honey, sugar, butter, for about 10 minutes until boils and sugar is dissolved-smooth.
2. Put in almonds and sesame.
3. Keep stirring constantly with wooden spoon over medium heat (continues to boil) until almonds change color on end (from white to brownish).
4. When almonds turn brown, it is done.
5. On large wooden cutting board rub butter generously over entire board.
6. Pour hot mixture onto board and with wooden spoon spread out thin evenly.
7. After spreading cut long lines in angles, be carefully it may still be hot. (Do not let mixture get hard before cutting!)
8. Place giugiulena pieces on wax paper and let dry for about 4 hours.
9. After dried completely place in tins layered with wax paper and store in cool place. Keeps 1 year.

SERVES 30 PEOPLE

 GIUGIULENA (JOO-JOO-LEH-NAH) IS ONE OF THE MANY SWEETS ITALIANS MAKE AROUND CHRISTMAS.

These sesame-almond candies are a testament to Sicily's history and multicultural pedigree. As has been stated by food historians and linguists, both modern Spanish "ajonjoli" and giugiulena are from a less common medieval Arabic name for sesame — "juljulaan". "Juljul" means a small bell, a jingle bell. "Al-jonjolin" was the current word in Moorish Spain. Hence, the Spanish word for sesame, ajonjoli. A sesame blossom looks like a small bell and a dry sesame seed capsule rattles. Variations of giugiulena are widespread throughout the Mediterranean.

Itza so easy!

Holiday drinks... thank you Gina A., for showing me how to make this dream come true.

Treats & Drinks

Aunt Audrey's Scramble

Orangecello

Dorothy Pastor's Chocolate Clusters

Chocolate Clusters – Dorothy Pastor NYC

INGREDIENTS:

2 (6 oz) pkg butterscotch morsels
1 (6 oz) pkg Hershey sweet morsels (light or dark)
1 (6 oz) can cashews (any nut of your preference can be used)
1 (3 oz) can Chinese noodles

DIRECTIONS:

1. Melt first two ingredients stirring constantly.
2. Add nuts and noodles to coat.
3. Spoon tsp size quantity onto wax paper that has been placed on cookie tray.
4. Refrigerate until they become hard.
5. Remove from refrigerator and store in tins lined with wax paper in a cool place.

Note: Can be made ahead to enjoy for the Holidays or for guests coming to visit.

MAKES 30 PIECES

Caramelized Corn – Francesca Modica Doubleday

Italian neighbor extraordinaire.

INGREDIENTS:

8 cups popped popcorn
1 cup peanuts (optional)
¾ cup brown sugar
3 TBS corn syrup
⅓ cup butter
¼ tsp baking soda

DIRECTIONS:

1. In a saucepan, heat brown sugar, corn syrup and butter, bring to a boil.
2. Cover and cook at a boil for 5 minutes.
3. Remove from heat.
4. Add baking soda.
5. Pour over popcorn and peanuts if using, mix well.
6. Bake on a large cookie sheet at 300° for 15 minutes.
7. Stir and remove to parchment paper to let cool.

Note: Can be stored in airtight containers.

SERVES 10-12

Aunt Fran's Delicious Christmas Nuts

INGREDIENTS:

1 ½ cup (1 lb) dry roasted peanuts
1 ½ cup walnuts or pecans
½ cup sugar
1 TBS pumpkin pie spice
1 egg white and 1 tsp water beaten until white

DIRECTIONS:

1. Mix nuts, sugar, and pumpkin spice together in a bowl.
2. Add beaten egg white, mix well.
3. Butter a large cookie sheet and place nuts on sheet.
4. Bake in 250° gas or 200° electric oven.
5. Cook 20-30 minutes.
6. Remove from oven and let cool completely.
Store in tins or jars.

SERVES 15-20

Friends that become family for life.

Aunt Audrey's Scramble

INGREDIENTS:

2 lbs mixed salted nuts
1 (12 oz) pkg of wheat chex
1 (6 ½ oz) of rice chex
1 (10 ½ oz) pkg cheerios
1 (6 ½ oz) pkg pretzel bits
1 (5 ¼ oz) pkg slim pretzel sticks
2 cups of peanut oil or vegetable oil
2 TBS Worcestershire sauce
1 TBS garlic salt
1 TBS Lawry's seasoned salt

DIRECTIONS:

1. In large roaster combine nuts, cereals, and pretzels.
2. In medium sized bowl combine oil, Worcestershire sauce, garlic salt, Lawry's salt, and mix well.
3. Pour over ingredients in roaster, coating well.
4. Bake at 250° for 2 hours stirring and turning mixture with wooden spoon every 15-20 minutes.
5. Makes about 8 quarts.

Note: When done turn off oven, open door and let cool before storing. Stores well in cookie tins. Great for parties and festivities!

MAKES 8 QUARTS

This makes a wonderful gift for the holidays.

Wassail Drink – Shakespearean Holiday Drink

INGREDIENTS:

1 gallon of apple cider
2 oranges, no skins
Handful of whole cloves, stuck into the oranges
6 cinnamon sticks

DIRECTIONS:

1. Place ingredients in large pot on stove and simmer for 6-8 hours.

This can be served with your favorite liquor such as rum or bourbon. Best served in large punch bowl.

Note: This is also delicious for the under 21 group with no liquor.

SERVES 30-35 PEOPLE

Russian Tea

Because I am blessed with a Russian daughter in-law.

INGREDIENTS:

2 cups tang
½ cup instant tea
1 tsp cinnamon
¼ cup sugar
½ tsp ground cloves
1 pkg of dry lemonade mix

DIRECTIONS:

1. Mix dry ingredients together and store in a sealed jar or can.
2. Use 1 or 2 tsp per cup of boiling water for a delicious warm tea. Or chill for iced tea.

Russian tea goes great with Biscotti!

Mary Finnecharo's Celebration Drink

INGREDIENTS:

3 cans of frozen pink lemonade
6 cans of water
3 cans of rum

DIRECTIONS:

1. Mix together and put into freezer for at least 8 hours.
2. Serve in martini glasses with an orange slice or cherry or both.

SERVES 10-12

Mary was my Godmother and made me feel special and cherished. With a twinkle in her eye, she gave me this fun drink.

Daiquiri

INGREDIENTS:

2 cups dark rum
1 ½ cups of fresh lime juice
2 cups of sugar syrup (1 cup water and 1 cup sugar melted together)
1 qt container

DIRECTIONS:

1. Mix all ingredients together in container.
2. Garnish with slices of lime.

SERVES 10-12

Ramos Fizz – Uncle Sam's

Fabulous beverage for brunches.

INGREDIENTS:

1 oz sweet and sour lemon juice
1 ½ oz milk
1 egg white
1 tsp powdered sugar
1 oz of gin
4 dashes of Orange Flower Water
1-2 drops vanilla
Crushed ice

DIRECTIONS:

1. Using blender, place above ingredients.
2. Blend until frothy, about 1 minute.
3. Use 1 handful of crush ice in the process.
4. Serve in 8 oz glasses.

Note: Use equal amounts of above ingredients to double and triple.

Orangecello

INGREDIENTS:

7 medium navel oranges
1 bottle vodka (750 mg)
2 ½ cups water
1 ½ cups sugar

DIRECTIONS:

1. Using a vegetable peeler, remove peels from the oranges in long strips. Reserve the oranges for another use (like making Sicilian orange salad).
2. Using a sharp knife, trim away the white pith and discard.
3. Place the orange peels in a 2 qt pitcher or a large glass bowl.
4. Pour vodka over peels; cover with plastic wrap.
5. Steep the orange peels in the vodka for 4 days at room temperature.

After 4 days:
1. In a medium saucepan, combine the water and sugar over medium heat.
2. Simmer for 5 minutes, stirring occasionally until the sugar has completely dissolved.
3. Remove the pan from heat and allow the syrup to cool, about 20 minutes.
4. Pour the syrup over the vodka mixture, cover again, let stand at room temperature overnight.
5. Strain the orangecello through a mesh strainer, discarding the peels.
6. Transfer the orangecello into bottles, seal with the bottles and refrigerate until cold.

MAKES 3 QUARTS
Can be kept in refrigerator for a month and in freezer indefinitely.

Breakfast

BONUS SECTION

Asparagus Frittata

Mom's Famous Coffee Cake

Zucchini Cake

"Breakfast"
The Most Important Meal of the Day

Nana's Pancakes

INGREDIENTS:

2 eggs (separate: beat whites to a peak and beat the yolk with 2 TBS oil and pinch of salt)
1 tsp sugar
1 ½ tsp baking powder
¼ tsp baking soda
1 ½ cup of milk
1 ½ cup of flour

DIRECTIONS:

1. Mix everything but egg whites, fold in whites at the end (Do not blend completely).
2. Rub griddle with oil and cook on medium heat.

SERVES 4-6

Mom's Famous Coffee Cake

INGREDIENTS FOR CAKE:

¼ lb of butter (1 stick)
1 cup of sugar
2 eggs beaten lightly
1 tsp baking soda
1 (8 oz) carton sour cream
1 ½ cup of sifted flour
1 ½ tsp baking powder (add baking powder last)
1 tsp vanilla
Baking pan with hole in the center (greased and floured with butter)

INGREDIENTS FOR FILLING AND TOPPING:

¼ cup of sugar
1 TBS cinnamon
½ cup chopped walnuts
In a bowl mix all together and set aside.

DIRECTIONS FOR CAKE:

1. Beat together butter, sugar, and eggs.
2. In a separate small bowl add baking soda and sour cream, let rise.
3. Slowly add flour to step 1.
4. Add sour cream mixture and vanilla.
5. Last add baking powder and blend.
6. Pour half of batter in prepared baking pan.
7. Sprinkle half of filling on batter.
8. Pour rest of batter into the pan and sprinkle remaining filling on top.
9. Bake at 350° in center of oven for 30 minutes.
10. Leave in open oven 20 minutes. Then remove.
11. Flip over onto plate and enjoy!

SERVES 10-12

Asparagus Frittata

INGREDIENTS:

1 large bunch fresh asparagus (wash and slice down the center 4 times then cut in half)
12 mushrooms, sliced
5 cloves of garlic, pressed
½ cup Italian parsley, pressed
¼ cup olive oil
Sea salt and ground pepper to taste
6-8 large eggs
½ cup grated Romano cheese

DIRECTIONS:

1. Sauté all of the above except eggs and cheese, until liquid is absorbed and asparagus is tender.
2. This can be prepared ahead of time and refrigerated.
3. In a separate bowl, beat eggs until foamy and add ½ tsp of salt
4. In a large stick free skillet, place asparagus mixture and warm on low heat, adding 1 TBS of olive oil to the skillet when warming.
5. Add the beaten eggs, DO NOT MIX.
6. Sprinkle with grated cheese and cover with lid.
7. On lowest heat cook until eggs are set.
8. Slied onto large plate, slice in pie slices or any way you like.

SERVES 10-12

Note: This can be wonderful for brunches, appetizer, or vegetable. So good!

Fresh Tomato Tart

INGREDIENTS:

1 large refrigerated pie crust
2 cups shredded Monterey jack cheese
3 TBS fresh basil, chopped
4 medium fresh tomatoes
1 ½ TBS virgin olive oil
2 twists fresh cracked black pepper

DIRECTIONS:

1. Put pie crust in 10inch pie pan or tart pan.
2. Generously prick the bottom and sides with fork.
3. Bake at 400° for 5-6 minutes and remove from oven.
4. Sprinkle cheese evenly into shell top with basil.
5. Arrange tomatoes on top of basil and brush with olive oil.
6. Bake at 400° for 30-40 minutes.
7. Remove from oven and garnish with fresh basil.

SERVES 8-9

Mom's Impossible Quiche

No pie crust, just impossible deliciousness for breakfast or lunch.

INGREDIENTS:

12 slices bacon (about ½ lb) crisply fried and crumbled
1 cup shredded Swiss cheese (about 4 oz)
⅓ cup onion, finely chopped
2 cups of milk
½ cup of Bisquick baking mix
4 eggs
¼ tsp salt
1/8th tsp pepper

DIRECTIONS:

1. Preheat oven 350°.
2. Lightly grease a 9 or 10-inch pie plate with butter.
3. Sprinkle bacon, cheese, and onion evenly over the bottom of pie plate.
4. Place the remaining ingredients in blender, cover, and blend on high speed for 1 minute.
5. Pour into pie plate and bake until golden brown and the knife inserted in the center comes out clean (50-55 minutes).
6. Let stand for 5 minutes before cutting.

SERVES 6

Smoked Salmon Delight by Marrietta

INGREDIENTS:

1 filet of smoked salmon
4 chopped green onions
1 tsp grated lemon reined
2 TBS olive oil
Juice of 1 lemon

CONDIMENTS:

Soft cream cheese
Rye bread or small bagels

DIRECTIONS:

1. Chop salmon and add all of the ingredients.
2. Mix with wooden spoon.
3. Serve with cream cheese to spread on bread.
4. A spoonful of salmon on top.

Mmmmm Good!

SERVES 8

Prosciutto with Fresh Pear or Fresh Cantaloupe

INGREDIENTS:

2 large bosc pears, peeled and cored, slice each pear in 8 long wedges
½ cantaloupe, peeled and sliced in 16 long wedges
8 oz thin sliced parma prosciutto, enough for 1 slice per piece of fruit

DIRECTIONS:

1. Wrap sliced of prosciutto around each slice of fruit, can be kept together with a toothpick.
2. Place on platter and serve immediately.

SERVES 4-6

Zucchini Cake

INGREDIENTS:

2 cups of flour
2 cups of sugar
1 generous cup of oil
2 eggs
Hand beat the above together
In separate bowl:
3 cups zucchini, grated
1 tsp salt
1 cup of walnuts, chopped
1 (6 oz) bag chocolate chips
2 tsp baking soda

DIRECTIONS:

1. Add all ingredients together and mix my hand.
2. Lightly butter and flour cake pan.
3. Pour cake mixture into pan.
4. Bake 350° for 50 minutes. Check to make sure toothpick comes out clean.
5. Remove from oven and let cool.

FROSTING INGREDIENTS:

1 small pkg Philadelphia cream cheese
½ stick butter
½ to ¾ box of powdered sugar
2 tsp vanilla
Mix all together to make a smooth frosting. When cake is cool, frost the cake.

MAKES 2 LOAVES OR 1 OBLONG PAN

Italian Biscotti

Aunt Sara Amato, my dad's sister.

INGREDIENTS:

5 cups of flour
1 ½ cup sifted powdered sugar
½ tsp salt
6 tsp baking powder
1 cup of butter
3 eggs
1 TBS almond flavoring
½ tsp vanilla
6 drops of food coloring if desired

DIRECTIONS:

1. In a large bowl sift dry ingredients and cut in butter.
2. With hands make a well.
3. Add eggs, flavoring, and color. (If sticky add more flour, if too stiff 1 TBS milk)
4. Roll dough into rope, ½ inch thick. Cut 1½-inch pieces.
5. Place pieces on greased cookie sheet.
6. Bake at 375 for 8-10 minutest, or until lightly brown.
7. Cool for 5 minutes and glaze with powdered sugar icing.

MAKES 6 DOZEN

Note: For powdered sugar icing refer to Ricotta Cookie Biscotti recipe.

These wonderful cookies come in all shapes and sizes. Recipes are tweaked as each generation perfects!

Ricotta Cookie Biscotti

Christmas or Easter favorites.

INGREDIENTS:

2 cups sugar
1 cup of butter softened
1 (15oz) container of ricotta cheese
2 tsp vanilla
2 large eggs
(Mix the above ingredients with beater until fluffy on low speed)
4 cups flour
2 TBS baking powder
1 tsp salt
(Mix together flour, baking powder and salt. Then add on medium speed to the above. Dough will form.)

INGREDIENTS FOR FROSTING:

1 ½ cup powder sugar
3 TBS milk (as needed)
Food color or sprinkles or both

DIRECTIONS:

1. On ungreased cookie sheet, place 1 level TBS dough 2 inches apart.
2. Bake 350° for 15 minutes. Cookies are soft.
3. Remove and let cool before adding frosting.

MAKES 5 DOZEN

Banana Cookies – Deanna's

INGREDIENTS:

2 sticks of butter
1 cup granulated sugar
1 cup dark brown sugar
2 eggs
¼ cup sour cream
2-3 bananas depending on size
1 tsp baking soda
1 tsp vanilla
3 ¼ cup of flour
½ cup chopped walnuts (optional)

DIRECTIONS:

1. Mix butter, eggs, sugar, sour cream, vanilla, baking soda, and bananas.
2. Slowly add dried ingredients to mix and blend.
3. Add nuts if using.
4. On buttered cookie sheet place tablespoon size drop of batter leaving space between for cookie to expand.
5. Bake at 350° for 10-12 minutes.
6. Remove and let cool.

FROSTING INGREDIENTS:

1 (8oz) pkg cream cheese
1 stick of butter
1 ¾ pound of powdered sugar
Mix together until smooth.

Note: This frosting can be frozen and used for another time.

MAKES 5 DOZEN

Homemade Ricotta

INGREDIENTS:

1 gallon whole non-homogenized milk (available at health food stores)
4 cups cultured whole-milk buttermilk
Salt

DIRECTIONS:

1. Combine the milk and buttermilk in a large, heavy-bottomed pot and slowly heat, stirring occasionally, until the mixture reaches 180°.
2. Remove the pot from the heat and let sit for 30 minutes to allow the curds to form. Do not stir or the ricotta will have a grainy, thin texture.
3. Line a colander with a double layer of butter muslin.
4. Carefully pour or ladle the curds into the colander and let drain for an hour or two, depending on how dry you want your ricotta.
5. When the ricotta has drained, transfer it to a bowl and break up the curds by stirring.
6. Add salt to taste.
7. Use right away or store, covered, in the refrigerator for up to a week.

MAKES 2 QUARTS

Chocolate Biscotti "Thathos"

Cousin Mary Lou Bonafide-Garnett

INGREDIENTS:

4 cups of flour
1 cup of sugar
1 tsp almond flavoring
3 heaping tsp baking powder
1 heaping tsp cinnamon
½ tsp salt
½ tsp ground cloves
¾ cup coco
1 cup Crisco + 2 heaping TBS
1 cup of milk (if needed add more)
3 eggs
1 cup chopped walnuts

DIRECTIONS:

1. In mix master, cream, sugar, shortening, and eggs.
2. Add cinnamon, salt, cloves, baking powder, and coco to flour. Mix well.
3. Alternate milk and flour into mixer.
4. Add nuts last, stirring with spoon.
5. On lightly greased cookie sheet, drop 1 TBS of batter about 2 inches apart.
6. Bake at 350° for 15 minutes until bottoms are light brown. Do not overcook.

FROSTING:

½ lb box of powdered sugar
2 TBS warm water and any flavor you choose (rum is good)
Add a little cocoa if you want frosting to be chocolate.
Make sure frosting is thin, more water may be added as needed.
Make frosting in 6½ quart pan, put a dozen biscotti at a time, stir fast, don't break and place on wax paper to dry. Continue until all are frosted.

MAKES 75

Note: This frosting without cocoa can be used on any biscotti. Double recipe if more frosting is needed.

 Mary Lou is a fabulous cook and she makes all the traditional treats, thus passing down the legacy to her family.

Casatte

This treat is usually made at Easter, but tastes good anytime of the year!

INGREDIENTS FOR DOUGH:

Mix together in mix master
1 ¼ cup Crisco
1 ¼ cup sugar
6 eggs
3 tsp vanilla
½ cup of milk
¼ cup of water
In a bowl sift all together:
6 cups flour
1 tsp salt
4 tsp baking powder
Pour liquid ingredients into flour, mix thoroughly; it will form a nice ball of dough. Set aside with towel over dough.

INGREDIENTS FOR FILLING:

6 lbs ricotta
2 cups sugar
10 large eggs
4 tsp cinnamon
1 ½ tsp vanilla
Mix all together in mix master until lumps are small.

NEEDED:

1 large board to roll dough out
4 cupcake pans
2 lb lid from coffee can (this size makes the perfect cupcake)
1 rolling pin

DIRECTIONS:

1. Sprinkle flour on the board.
2. Take half of the dough, cut in half, roll out each section enough to fill 1 cupcake pan. Cutting with the lid. * Tip: spray cupcake pan with Pam before placing dough in tin.
3. Flute the edges of dough.
4. Fill dough with ricotta filling to the very top. Sprinkle with cinnamon.
5. Bake at 400° for 25 minutes. Note: cupcakes should easily slip out of tin.

MAKES 48 CUPCAKES

This recipe can be doubled by making entirely separate batch. These can also be frozen in airtight containers and taken out even 1 at a time for a delicious morning breakfast.

Recipe Index

Apple Crisp 96
Apple Pie 95
Apricot Glazed Hens 68
Apricot Pie 95
Asparagus Frittata 113
Banana Cookies 117
Beets Italian Style 24
Blue Cheese Dip 10
Broccoli Fugati 26
Broccoli w/ Sautéed Garlic and Mushroom 26
Cannellini Ham Bone Soup 39
Cannoli 101
Caramelized Corn 106
Caramelized Onions 28
Casatte 119
Cauliflower Soup 38
Celebration Drink 109
Cheese Sauce 45
Cheesecake 99
Chicken Cacciatore 66
Chicken Piccata 64
Chocolate Biscotti "Thathos" 118
Chocolate Clusters 106
Christmas Fruitcake 97
Christmas Nuts 107
Clam Pasta 47
Clam Pasta, White Sauce 46
Clam Sauce – Red 47
Coffee Cake 112
Cornish Hens with White Grapes 62
Crab Supper Pie 60
Curing Black Olives 88
Curing Green Olives 88
Daiquiri 109
Devils Food Mayonnaise Cake 96
Eggplant With Parmesan Béchamel Sauce .. 30
Escargot 11
Fava Beans and Pork Chops 80
Fettuccine Primavera 48
Fresh Basil Dressing 16
Fresh Tomato and Onion
Salad – Sicilian Style 19
Fresh Tomato Tart 113
Fried Peppers with Tomato and Onions –
"Bibi Cu Skoucha" 27
Giugiulena 102
Gnocchi 44
Gnoccholi 94
Gorgonzola Sauce 45
Green Beans w/ Garlic, Vinegar, and Mint . 28
Green Goddess Dressing 16
Hamburger and Rice Turkey Stuffing 72
Hoisin Chicken 64
Holiday Turkey 70
Homemade Ricotta 117
Hot Artichoke Dip 11
Hot Hamburger Sandwiches 72
Impossible Quiche 114
Italian Biscotti 116
Italian Chicken Soup 36
Italian Cracked Olives 89
Italian Dressing 16
Italian Minestrone Soup 37
Italian Sausage 84
Italian Stew in Slow Cooker 78
Italian Wedding Soup 36
Leg of Lamb 79
Leg of Lamb or Lamb Shanks 79
Lemon Prawns over Linguine 46
Lentils 39
Liathina (Head Cheese) 84
Marinated Chicken Breasts Sicilian Style 62
Marinated Fresh Dungeness Crab 59
Marinated Mozzarella 17
Marinated Salami & Tomato Antipasto 10
Mashed Potatoes Ahead 32
Meat Bolognese 55
Meat Ravioli 49
Meatballs 71
Muffaletta 12
Nebraska Runzas 74
New England Clam Chowder 40
Orangecello 110
Osso Buco 81
Oven Fried Chicken 63
Pancakes 112
Pasta With Anchovies 56
Pastari 73
Peach or Blackberry Cobbler 94
Pesto Basil Sauce 53
Pickled Hot Banana Peppers 85
Pizza Dough 90
Prosciutto with Fresh Pear or Cantaloupe 115
Ramos Fizz 110
Raspberry Jell-O Mold 18
Red Roasted Potatoes 33
Ricotta Cookie Biscotti 116
Ricotta Ravioli 51
Roasted Peppers 27
Russian Tea 108
Sasa "Quick Sauce" – Meatless 52
Sausage Bolognese 55
Scramble 107
Sfingi 100
Shepherd's Pie 75
Sicilian Asparagus Stew 42
Sicilian Baby Back Ribs 80
Sicilian Breaded Chicken 69
Sicilian Breaded Prawns 59
Sicilian Fausomauro (Braciole) 78
Sicilian Fish and Olives 58
Sicilian Italian Potato Salad 31
Sicilian Orange Salad 18
Sicilian Pasta, Chicken, and Peas 63
Sicilian Tripe – 2 Ways 92
Sicilian Vegetable Caviar 25
Sicilian White Fish in Light Tomato Sauce . 58
Smashed Potatoes w/ Garlic and Parsley 33
Smoked Salmon Delight 114
Spaghetti Carbonara 53
Spicy Shrimp Pizza 60
Spinach Soup 38
Stuffed Artichokes 24
Stuffed Eggplant 23
Stuffed Manicotti 54
Stuffed Zucchini 25
Sugo 50
Sweet Potato Mash 32
Tomato & Rustic Bread Salad 14
Tournedo Strip 77
Tri-Tip – Champagne Mushroom Sauce 77
Vodka Cream Pasta Sauce 52
Wassail Drink –
Shakespearean Holiday Drink 108
Watermelon Pickles 85
Zabaione 97
Zucchini Cake 115
Zucchini Soup 40

www.ingramcontent.com/pod-product-compliance
Lightning Source LLC
Chambersburg PA
CBHW061117170426
43199CB00026B/2952